A Life's Canvas

A Life's Canvas

On changes, chances and choices

A M GUTIERREZ JEFFE

CP

THE CHOIR PRESS

First published in the United Kingdom in 2022 by
The Choir Press

ISBN 978-1-78963-298-9

To God, my strength. My Family who are my rock that I hold so dear. My Hubby, who is my teammate. My friends who keep me steady. And grandma Epifania who is walking alongside with my Shadow in heaven watching over us.

And I dedicate this to YOU reading this, that in some way may help you sketch your own canvas in life.

Lyna,

We find that our journey has it's purpose...

Thank you for taking that journey with me.

always,

Ana

First thoughts are the everyday thoughts,
Everyone has those.
Second thoughts are the thoughts you think about the way
you think,
People who enjoy thinking those.
Third thoughts are thoughts that watch the world and think
all by themselves.
They are rare, and often troublesome.

Tiffany Aching in "A Hat Full of Sky" (Pratchett, 2005)

When Spring Comes

The dawn has come and the night slowly ended—
The stillness of the world has brought a sublime calmness—
The subtlety of the wind stroking the branches of the trees—
The birds chirped in harmony as they nestled in comfort—
Day has emerged, now the sun has risen to its throne—
As the moon bade farewell to its rest with a promise for later.

My sleepy mind is awakened by the sweet melody of the morning—
I tossed and turned, feeling lazy to get up—
My cosy bed cuing me to stay with its warmth—
I curled under the sheets, cuddled my pillow for some console—
Though my eyes still shut, my thoughts had strayed away—
Beckoning my senses to open up and stretch out—
I blinked, then for a moment I found myself saying, "This is going to be a
    good day!"

Daylight has now slowly welcomed its grace—
The ray lit my room with colours of perfection—
Clocks had chimed and tic-toc to its fitting time—
Busy streets, horns and beeps signals a start of another day—
People in their "Hellos" and "Goodbyes", I can imagine their waves and
    smiles—
One portrait of an inspiring break of a new season on a one fine day.

In a spur, I smiled, hopped and whistled a happy tune—
I drew my curtains to look out, to relish the day—
The fresh air wiped my face with an awakening—
The soft rays of light from the morning sun bathe me with newness—
The birds on the treetop with their harmony nestled in my
    thoughts—
Today, I am starting life with a hope that it's all going to be OK!

The trees are starting to show its shade of green, I noticed—
Flowers blossomed to its peak, an exquisite site to see—
Bees and ladybirds passing, dancing and prancing for a sip of sweetness to
    its risen buds—
The smell of the freshly cut grass sank deeply into my senses—
And the air blowing my thoughts anew with zest—
While the sun stretched its magnificent vigour, I felt it cuddling me to safety.

I summoned my thoughts back to reality, facing a promise of a better
    day—
As I walked with inspiration, still caught and entangled in a
    daydream—
I gathered and scrapped all the picturesque stories to tell and
    live by—
Of one springtime where new things cast new beginnings—
For yet another day, another horizon, another hope for the next spring time!

April 2010

Show Me How to Breathe

Show me how to breathe
Let the blood flow and run through the depths of my veins
Let the fluid wash away my fears, my pain
Let its colour cover my life filled with sorrow
And let every drop steal away a joy to borrow.

Show me how to breathe
Let the air blow away my anguish, my lonely soul
Let me inhale courage, dare my existence howl
Let the strength of your spirit engulf my sighs
And exhale all the hurt and ruins of my cries.

Show me how to breathe
Let your pureness banish the night and replace it with light
Let your faith cloak me with a hope to live ignite
Let your promise guide me when nothing seems to go right or real
And dispel my burden with your gentle embrace and your compassion to
    heal.

Show me how to breathe
Let your kindness nurture my silent whisper, be my voice
Let your breath taking candour capture my troubled choice
Let your inspiration be my field of roses in the prairies of life
And your will redeem me from a faded strife.

Show me how to breathe
When frustrations and defeat has weakened me
When my dreams and aspirations have crushed as far your eyes can see
Cuddle me with your love, your cherished passion
And cradle me tight in your arms like you never let go of your possession.

Thank you. Mama
May 2010

Amazing Graces

The sun starts to rise to its glory
The squirrels running towards the trees with nuts to bury
As birds in choir hum their morning song
Trees are dancing to the tune with branches swinging along
I tapped my feet, snapped my fingers created lyrics to the song
Come sing with me, and feel the rhythm and beat the gong.

Good morning sun, rising bright above the skies
Today has come, a time to seek our blessings high
Yesterday is past, and tomorrow is meant for something new
Today is today, leaves are green . . . a smell of morning dew.

Fly high we go, dreams to find and grow
Faith and hope wrapped in my heart with love to sow
Amazing graces are sent to me with more blessings bind
With a lock and key, a treasure of true happiness to find.

August 2010

Today

Dewdrops filling the flowers in bloom
The cool breeze subtle the morning sun's loom
Misty leaves shimmer when touched by its rays
The smell of freshness claiming the day.
The morning greets the earth with a smile

Just saying hello, how do you do and waving goodbye
Off for a day's task and the morning's rush
A day to fill an empty and half-filled cup.
Whenever or however, there is work to be done

For the sun continues to shine and soon will be gone
Just like the changing colours of the leaves from green, yellow, orange to
     crisp brown
Looking down at each passer-by with a sweet smile and never a frown.

As the day slowly filters to its own special accord
And the tasks are complete, the day's rush is filled and endured   –
Just look up and watch the majestic sun setting above the orange sky
For a moment to cherish of how today has ended as time goes by.

Sept. 2010

An Angel without Wings

In my moment of silent cries
In my clouded tears and futile lies
In between the sobs and sighs
In my surrender and weakened demise
An unspoken prayer is heeded by my side.

In my frailty, I have found defence
In my notion of limitations, I have seen sense
In my hopelessness, I have gathered strength
In my lost faith, came back a joyful spirit sent
A wilful prayer is whispered by my side.

In my anxious mind, I have drawn steadfast thoughts
In my trembled heart, someone have battled and fought
In my agonising wait, I am cuddled with courage
In my pessimism, I have collected love from a mileage
And a pure heartfelt prayer is heard by my side.

In my waiting hour, I have held a zealous hand
In my moment of anticipation, I am wrapped with trusted bond
In my chance of impatience, I am sheltered with a safe embrace
In my time of great relief, I am hushed with a promise of solace
Then there appeared an angel with a grateful smile to relish by my side.

Oct 2010

If Ever …

If ever …
I meet you somewhere, someday, somehow
Your face will light up with such tender avow
Your eyes will be looking – searching well for a mile
But all I will see is your gentle sweet smile.

If ever …
You say "Hello" just once
I will be hearing your heart in every bounce
And when I say your name with a blush
Your stare will find my soul in a flash.

If ever …
The right words are hard to find
Silence shall hold our thoughts entwined
With every moment of laughter we steal to share
A time and space shall be seized to spare.

If ever …
There will come a time to a broken promise
Please think it is not the intention, I surmise
For the pain that you shall have and feel
Is the hurt I will keep that no one can heal.

If ever …
A day will become a view of tomorrow
Remember only time is there for us to borrow
For no matter what and no matter how every moment's chance
You know where I am, a day you'll be finding me again – in a moment's
   glance.

Oct 2010

Thank You

The gentle caress engulfs my thoughts into my soul
Hushing to ease the unsettling night
Arms ready to hold and cuddle tight
No matter how that every moment is seized to rest
Keeping that promise of warmth and safe embrace.

You are the strength in my every cry of pain
One hush and whisper "I'm here" . . . voice of a whispered prayer
Until I fall into a calm sleep – I am wrapped with a vow to never let go until I
    awake.

Dec 2010

You and Me

You and me, serendipity met
Me and you, we simply connect
You and me, in our eyes we see
Me and you, felt it meant to be
You and me, find in each other's arms
Me and you, together safe from harm
You and me, discover each other's life
Me and you, create each other's light
You and me, found strength in each other's weakness
Me and you, bind courage with gentleness
You and me, made a wish and a dream
Me and you, a pinkie swear as it may seem
You and me, together found love
Me and you, if there's forever vowed love
You and me, in every journey we take
Me and you, will make that journey with faith.

Dec 2010

When I'm Missing You

When I'm missing you
I have my hand on my heart
I'd listen to every beat from the start
I'd close my eyes to make me feel
To see your face and see you smile for real.

When I'm missing you
I'd imagine tracing your face and sigh
Your eyes I'd be searching to drift me by
Your stare would be a comfort like I'm right next to you
With your soul reaching mine to carry me through.

When I'm missing you
I'd remember how we giggle and laugh
And when I do, I can't help myself but hop
I'd hear you tell me off "Hey no hopping"
My heart just swears it is really your voice I'm missing.

When I'm missing you
I would listen and sing the love we keep
It's the lullaby song you sing me to sleep
And tonight I lay in bed alone, I cry
I know I've promised no tears,
Darling I'm sorry I did try.

Dec 2010

One Winter Morning

The call of the birds started to sound in resonance
The croaks of the frogs across the lake hummed in unison
The soft blow of the wind brushed a hymn of silence
The trees bend and swayed with their arms enfold
As the moon bade farewell to its rest
The sun rose to its place it felt like a song and a melody of a new
    beginning.

The dew caressed the leaves as it dropped from one to another
The smell of a winter's morning fills an enchantment
The gush of the breeze tingled my senses
The softness of the light gently touching my skin
There in my solace, I peered thru my thoughts
To the depths of my being, I searched for something from a somewhere.

Beyond my dreams, I felt doubts. I felt my fears
In my faith, somehow I still craved for some disappointments
In my determination, I can sense faults and failures
In my confidence, seemed my self-esteem dropped to its lowest
That at a point in time my challenges may not be fought
That at some time my luck may have changed.

The thought of losing crept down my veins
The sounds of defeat have drowned my spirit
The echoes of courage have become hallow
It blocked my grip for survival, showing my pitfalls
My inner strength is becoming reckless to indulge in my weakness
Then my hope has stumbled and a cry of despair challenged my sanity.

At such turmoil, I started to redirect my vision
In my grief, I tried to look and searched deeper
There I saw a light inviting for a reformation
I sketched thru my future with a guided will
I trimmed my weakness with another hope for one more dream
That this time my faith will have reserves and will be a purpose.

11

The magic of each creation may be tangling and uncertain, I reckoned
The spell of each discovery may be surprising or confusing, I thought
Yet the moments of an extraordinary life spelt a different word
The spurs of time became the memories to be cherished
The spontaneity of each passing day became values of a journey
That thru it all I still have so much to thank for and live by.

As I resigned back to my solitude, in my tranquillity
I counted my blessings and ironed my optimism
I've realised, my pace just needed to slow down for a while
To notice the reasons and my existence
To log into the radical excerpts of a wonderful journey
That somewhere along the way, I may know you and then keep you.

As the world orbits the sun to its glory
As the day passes thru time and space
Here I am back again, in one cold winter morning
Reminiscing my seasons of laughter and tears
That after each day of either a joy or a pain, I have survived
Thru it all I have lived with a deep voice of love and loving.

Sometimes, I know I have to fail
Somewhere, I understand I have to fall
But somehow, I will learn and will gain a lesson
I will still dream, still have hope and continue to make wishes
Because I have you to believe in and to trust
That this time I shall stand and will fight to win again in the end.

For now, we may have parted ways and may have to leave
But remember, it's only a presence and it's just a physic
As spirits linger, there's always a smile that remains in painting
In thoughts ... in your heart I am to stay
Goodbyes are only said, for there will always be Hellos
If at any time and place, I am to meet you once again
It shall be a beginning and birth of another memory and another cycle
And it may be the same one winter morning again.

December 2010

When Tears Start to Fall

The gloom of the day seems favouring my thoughts,
The silent coldness of my existence enveloping time,
The beat of my heart aggravating every system,
The normal breaths becoming a painful sigh,
And the sweet gentle cuddle becoming a clench of hurt.

Looking back from a yesterday I thought I have done something right
Looking back from a past I thought I have made a better choice
Searching pass I seem to have followed a straight path
Searching slow I seem to have chosen a solemn promise or a broken vow
Yet I seem to have gained an endless worth of pain.

I closed my eyes to shut reality to form a dream
I clenched my fist to tighten my grip to another hope
I directed my soul to search for something happy . . . and serene
I imagined my heartbeat to find a connection somewhere
Then I wrestled at stopping the incoming flow of tears slowly dripping.

I fought for my system to find an equilibrium
To somehow find an outlet for the tears not to flow
I tried to pray harder this time to take away the hurt I feel
I summoned for miracles to block out such pain inside me
Just then, there seem nothing I can do and nothing seem to be alright.

I caved in to my thoughts and all the emotions stirring my world
I don't know if I can still hold on to each teardrop that falls
I'm afraid it may not be enough for me to stop at each pain
When the tears starts falling I may not be able to hope
Coz when a tear drops I know . . . I am already broken . . . I'm already
    drowned.

Dec 2010

Rainbow When It Rains

In my solitude, I hear the hum of raindrops falling by my window pane,
The warmth inside my room is in deep contrast from the outside world,
It seem the wind gushes through every depths of my thoughts,
The breeze trying to echo with my inner emotions,
The darkness of the clouds wanting to tremble my soul,
To overshadow with the glare of will entering in my solace.

In my own world candles are flickering with utmost grace,
The four corners of my room guarding for my safety,
The sound of stillness feeding my thoughts and filling my insights,
As realism paves in it sends wisdom through such a gloomy day,
Redirecting, redefining every strengths beyond the sharpness of each
    challenge,
Constructing new phases underneath failures and faults.

Peering outside the rain still dancing its way down the road,
The streetlamps remain standing even to threats of their existence,
The sun rays through the grey clouds to fulfil its purpose,
The gleam giving promise of another day entwined with hope,
Ducks flock in shapes of victory as their wings spread out with courage,
Trees come dancing in rhythm clenching deeply in their stance to keep on.

In my silence and at a moment tears trickled in and advancing a shout of
    letting go,
In my disappointments verge a bulk of hate in my point of weakness,
In my mind the thoughts of unworthiness settled in.. invoking my persistence,
In my heart emotions stirred loosening the grip of faith in my strength,
In my soul there stumbles my will weary and ready to quit. To give up,
My spirit drowned, drifting from the dream to grieve my real purpose.

The flicker of lights dazzled my sanctity with optimism on such down state,
The rain showed some signs of chivalry through the storm with pride,
Every drop signalling to find another chance of creation and reincarnate,
The wind blowing down my soul with a hope to move on and to believe,
Gazing through it I surmised in enchantment and discovery,
Looking further I've found more than just something inside me . . . a reason.

As the rain kept pouring underneath lie answers to my every questions,
Should it stop or not there still comes another day to make another dream,
Quietly I closed my eyes standing still ... I listened to the hymn of a new
    beginning with a smile,
As the day comes to an end. As the storm has calmed down,
I sensed lights have flashed an array of collars with a scent of fulfilment,
Through it all washed away are my sorrows. My pain and wipe my tears
    away,

Rainbows didn't hide when it rained. It was just there seizing up waiting for
    someone like me to find it and see,
That life in all its ups and downs, there is but another dream . . . another
    hope . . . another wish to make and just another way to love life again!

Dec 2010

15

A New Year's Love Letter

Dear God,

There is so much to thank for. I am grateful for all the joys of every laughter – they are extraordinary chances of every moment. Thank you for all the blessings – they are wonderful miracles of each day. Thank you for the little surprises – they are a reminder that life is beautiful.

So much has happened in the past year and I am sure more are coming this year. The trials which I see as small tests that made me who I am – stronger!

I ask for your forgiveness and tender mercy – for I am not perfect. Yet, in my imperfections, you design me uniquely – rare and special to you. Please show me wisdom to discern Your message – the sense to feel, the sensibility to understand and accept with an open mind.

Thank you for my family – my source of strength and inspiration. Thank you for my other half, my teammate – who gives me courage and my rock. Thank you for true friends – who are extra support to keep me steady. Please keep them safe and sound. Bless and protect them for they are my constant safe I hold dear in my heart – from the morning's first light to the night's moonlight and last star's shine. Thank you too for people I meet along the way – they became my friends and allies.

God, give me strength to lightly bear my pain. I have no plans as I live one day at a time, but let me see, hear and feel your presence – a precious calm to replace my worries and fears. Please take away my doubts – replace it with hope and faith seeing life's beautiful mysteries. And if your plans are better than mine and that of my dreams, please give me courage to live my life according to your will – with kindness and purpose. You know what is best for me and to you I trust my body and soul.

I do not know what is up ahead, but I believe you have something planned and have prepared a blueprint – far better than I deserve. And with faith within me, I can sense today is something special. As for tomorrow, it will be something wonderful.

And the future is one beautiful surprise worth living for with you leading the way.

Thank you, for loving me no matter what.

I love you,
Jan 2011

Butterfly Time to Fly

Butterfly time to fly . . .
From when you are a timid larva
From how you are a growing pretty caterpillar
From where you are in your shy cocoon
From what you are to become, a beauty!

Butterfly time to fly . . .
Open your eyes to the outside world
Gaze at the day of great wonder
Spread your wings in its beauty
Fly away to the new adventure.

Butterfly time to fly . . .
The horizon is inviting you with an open arm
To a journey of life and living
The world is waiting for you with a smile
For your dreams of faith and loving.

Butterfly time to fly . . .
Let your faith be your guide, your shield
Never lose your hope to a given chance
Breakaway and take the risk of destiny
It is your time to make a day of change.

Butterfly time to fly . . .
Let go of the rush of your fear
Take a chance to touch the sun and the skies
Now is the time to spread your wings and let be
Butterfly it is time to fly, please just fly away.

Birthday
Jan 2011

Wishful Starry Night

Starry starry night
Your sparkle beautiful and bright
Twinkle twinkle shine and light
Your glitter has set my sight.

Starry starry night
Little star dazzling with might
Twinkle twinkle alight
Your glow wraps my heart tight.

Starry starry night
You flash like a valiant knight
Twinkle twinkle up the skylights
Your glint flickers downright.

Starry starry night
Your shine sends my spirit to fight
Twinkle twinkle mighty than might
Your shimmer be my guide all through the night.

Starry starry night
Hear my wish I pray outright
Twinkle twinkle shining bright
May every wish come true tonight.

Jan 2011

A Walk in the Clouds

I stared blankly at the calming horizon
A glimpse silently captured every inch of my soul and my being
The picture glared with so much enchantment and sweetness
As my thoughts wandered off to places familiar from a lost memory
It captivated a feeling similar to a moment's past
There's a sunken feeling of emotion that hooked to an inner truth of the
    present.

I followed a path leading to a nowhere or a somewhere perhaps
The trail looked inviting as each step went farther
The more I stride, a discovery is witnessed and taken
The further I walked, an adventure of something stepped in
The closer I get, I saw old familiar faces in new fronts
Then came old thoughts becoming a new beginning.

The shimmer of the sun cupped my face with gentleness
The soft breeze of the day softly whispered like a song
The trees danced away in rhythm and stretched each branch with
    welcome
Begging me to hum an old familiar song in a different melody and phrase
And like a timid girl, I played old games with newness
To keep my spirits high, I've drawn pictures and traced beautiful smiles.

My thoughts travelled more and more to a distant shore
Feelings stirred up near with my heart beating with a prayer
As I continued the walk, I chose the aisle of challenge
There I've found something old in a somewhere and a someone to fill my
    faceless portraits
There created a pure soul of trust cloaked in purity
To stand the test to the never-ending wave of storm of weakness.

My journey, it seem not stopping as it moved in loops and twirls
Through the limits of my purpose I have wished and still hoped
Through the silver lines of my joys and sorrows, I've managed with courage
and love
Realising that thru rain or thru fire, I know I will survive and live
Knowing I have walked above clouds of strength, there stretched is a hand
of promise
And if my walk ends I am not worried nor scared
For thru it all I will find at the end the same path where there came you . . .
all over again.

Jan 2011

A Sky Seeker

The dawn breaks with a glimmer of the moonlight
The smell of fresh dew moistens the air
The soft breeze cupped my face – calm and collected
As I closed my eyes to embrace the new day
A smile traces like a serene hymn of my every heartbeat.

The vastness of the skies gently beckons my soul
The clouds jointly form a sign of welcome
The subtle flow of time searched my unguarded thoughts
As I take a deep breath to smell the call of a new journey
A hand tenderly held mine like a tranquil wind.

The sun begins to rise from its slumber
The ray tamed my anxious melancholy
The warmth graciously lifts and cuddles my sorrow
As I stared blankly to search for a new horizon
A long gaze glistens into my eyes like the radiant sun.

The day has begun calling a silent reverie
The sweet voice of comfort migrating high above like a bluebird
The flight of a songbird soaring like a free spirit towards the limitless sky
As I took a step to start seeking new adventures
Another step carefully moved beside me like a swift wing.

The world awaits as the skies surfaced in grandeur
The sound of the wind summons with a challenge
The call of the clouds signals to pursue my purpose
That as I answered with determined faith to a new destiny
A gentle voice uttered the words of strength and a promise – towards the
    summit skies.

Jan 2011

Like Songbird's Soul

A past – the memory . . .
A sad hymn can be heard with longing
There's a rhythm of bleak, broken note holding a tear and wanting
Every beat of the drum echoing through each dark clouds
And every word read a thousand folds of loneliness.
It's a songbird's soul lost, alone and encased.

The start – a meeting . . .
A lingering hum sounded like a magical symphony
The melody glimmers a tone reaching out for someone
Every string of the harp wavering a ray of light
And the language of life forms a written code of need
The songbird's soul reborn and holding on from falling.

From now – a voyage . . .
A whisper of a beautiful song filling the empty piece of the broken chord
There's a vibration hushing a chime with a promise of harmony
Every stroke of the keys charts an orchestra of a pulsating heart
And there – a poetry shapes in motion and depth
For the songbird's soul to rebuild the quietened voice.

And tomorrow – a destination . . .
A change of a new world and the start of a journey together
That every touch rhymes and speaks a sense of protection
Every blow of the trumpet casts a spell of safe haven
And in silence, a prayer is uttered with a gentle and moving harmony
A songbird's soul now finding the song of the heart – flying on the wings of
    ONE free spirit for the ONE pure love!

Feb 2011

The Symphony

The hum of the season, a sign of spring hue
A strum of the tree branch danced and sway
A beat of the leaves and bough fuse
Like a rhythm of wind, a soft breeze underlay.

The birds in its warm nest chirped and tweet
The bees buzzing towards each colourful blossom's arc
The caterpillars now soaring as elegant butterflies fleet
And the methodical ants slowly, gently in line marched.

While I watched this grandeur, just this very moment
My heart throbbed and beat like a drum
I closed my eyes to feel a deep fathom of thoughts
There I found a melody, a rhyme for me to sum.

Words softly formed like chains of notes
The pulse glided and flowing from within my soul
Then tenderly the lyrics becoming a story floats
The symphony, a serenade from my heart and a melody of my soul for you.

Mar 2011

Wish Upon

Wish upon a setting sun, to its colours of mystical solace
A painted wonder in awe of the masterpiece's charming face
The night's apparition, a horizon coveting to its place
The glitter of lights, strikes a captive embrace
For the day breaks to the sunset's welcome gaze.

Wish upon a moonlight, to its glow like bewildered jest
An enchanted refuge of a castle to its regal nest
The silver moon alluring to a craved comfort's rest
Haunting beacon that sparks the shadowy crest
For the evening yearns to linger a moment's request.

Wish upon a falling star, its twinkle and magical bid
A long for destiny, a true but surreal need
The mirage encompassing a safe haven for dream to heed
A radiant sparkle seizing the trembled faith whisper creed
For the dusk aspires the sanguine love's promise sealed.

Wish upon the sunrise, its ascend flashed in sublime
An urge for a miracle, a daring hope inclined
The luminescent spirit, a clasp devotion bind
That brilliantly calls and clutching a faltered soul to shine
For the dawn has persisted and dared to valiantly climb.

Wish upon the new day, it's a birth of the sun
A hunger for creation, a lustre of intuition began
The brightness of a sincere heart fastened with enjoined hands
The glare of sunbeam contain the toppled courage ends
For the cycle goes on like a wheel, a journey of another wish send.

Mar 2011

The Moonlight's Ballad

The sunset wrapped the day in animated colours
A scenic sight to end the day of rush and surge
While the moon starts rising to a crescendo of light
A spark of rhythm and drumbeat echoes along
Capturing the subdued soul of the daylight's hymn.

The resonant moon glare in the orbit's shanty
Painting a blaze of melancholic ambience and sweet sounds
A spellbinding lamp serenading the nightfall sublime
Its radiance filled the phantom and sombre eventide
Resigned to its full luminescent shaded chant.

Picturesque and salient, glows a poetic dream
An orchestra ignites the subtle hue to clear the day's air
The glare of twilight envelops a sensuous refrain
A portrait of harmony to a poignant lyrical reverie
Seducing sundown to a submissive solace of acoustic flight.

The kaleidoscope became a replica of a daydream's chord
Wholly, its gleam revives a sphere of the soothing cello
Flushed with a tune of divine tonic, glowing deeply into the skies
The bright silhouette uplifting the soul of a gloaming harp
It ignites the chorus resembling a graphic panorama of tinted rays.

The dusk glimmers to a resplendent arrangement of vividness
The soft tinge transfixing an acapella, savouring a dream
The lantern's flame, lavishly brightens the darkened space
Illuminating regally to its perfect charm and grace
Poised to play a lullaby . . . the ballad of the night's prayer and a melody of
    a heart's daze.

Apr 2011

From A Wishing Well

From a wishing well
I thought of something I long to feel
I thought of somewhere surreal
I thought somehow there's time to steal
And thought of someone holding me safely still.

From a wishing well
I dream of a life for faith to define
I dream of destiny's summit to climb
I dream of a solemn trust to bind
And dream of a lover's sonnet to find.

From a wishing well
I pray for a tight and sweet embrace
I pray to live in a serene place
I pray to see your tranquil sweet gaze
And pray to touch your gentle face.

From a wishing well
I hope for special moments to cease
I hope for a soft whisper of promise
I hope to hear your heart beat without a miss
And hope to feel your tender, sweet kiss.

From a wishing well
I wish to dream and keep your heart in mine to grow
I wish – a prayer to heal the past and happy memories to flow
I wish for our every hope be the guiding flame to glow
And from a wishing well I wish, "my heart you shall keep and love be
    contained by you alone."

Apr 2011

Hush

The silence has filled the dawn
As emptiness inhabits the room
There's a hollow curtain of serenity
And a thought sinks into nothingness
I sensed a quiet grasp of contentment.

In my solitude, I reviewed my thoughts
Maybe there is something there I can find
In my distinct bareness, I re-created my visions
Maybe there is somewhere that I can see
Yet, a blank canvas is what I set my eyes on.

I stared past the whiteness from a frame
Maybe I can fill the void with a speck
I looked deeper through its pale fabric
Maybe I will notice a trail of fragments
But all I can seize is a glimpse of shade.

From the shade, I drew a streak of colour
From the streak, I sketched the element of wonder
From the sketch, I drafted the facets of dream
From the draft, I composed the feature of imagination
Then in stillness, a loving gaze lulls me safely back to sleep . . . whispering
  "Hush baby hush, you're safe."

May 2011

A Cutting Edge

I woke up serene – in deep thoughts
The waking hour, a start of another day
The waking moment – a beginning of another challenge
The waking pause – a time to face with courage of what awaits me today.

In deep solitude – I started to ask, "Will I be able to make this?"
Reality bites, I said – maybe I will or maybe I won't.
If I make it – it is all good and it's going to feel great
And if I won't? – Stuff it, I will do it again!

With courage and in high spirits – I took a step
With hope and inspiration – I took the stride
On a cutting edge I may fail today – but I won't fall
With a cutting edge I can always take a lesson then say, "I can make it
    through on any given day."

June 2011

On a Summer day, when it comes …

The gentle light from my window woke me up
Its luminous ray softly cupped my face with tenderness
The heat felt warm – enough to stroke my skin
Its brightness bringing a new day – a new life
And the sparkle – promises a hope and a start of a one fine day.

Stretching with grateful fondness of my existence
I shivered at a possibility of a new day to dream
I whispered a prayer – a wish for a day of only simple things
With a happy thought – I ought to wish for angelic serendipities
All but a smile to greet the world of mystical shower of blessing is enough.

Silently, I pondered for a list to do today
In subdued thoughts, I see wonderful ideas to my meekness
In solitude, I re-discovered faith with a glimpse of certainty
My face lit in boldness – full of aspirations for the extraordinary
With a new start, I stepped out openly to embrace the beautiful life again.
Strolling along the paths, a shadow startled me

Doubts focused deeply but I withdrew from the sight
Yet I kept on with a shield of courage – redirecting to a better path
I stopped and felt frozen at a trace of a smile I see
Staring in curiosity – it's looking back with a question of daze.

From a distance – unmoved and in stillness I saw you
In your eyes – your stare leaving me breathless
In your smile – my heart beat like drums of the tribes
In your arms – I felt a strength of life and the warmth of safety
And in your touch – I sensed courage and a free spirit of love.

As you walked towards me – in amusement and playfulness
I felt a tingle that lingered through my spine
I seemed to have lost my balance as you walked closer and closer
Looking through my eyes, you searched for my soul
And as you held me in your arms, I knew I am never alone.

Leading to an open path – the trees danced in tune
As the sun scattered its blaze to possess the day
The rhythm of the breeze carried us to a magical place
With your heart guiding mine – a love in sweet surrender with trust
One summer, I will wake up with you to a real journey of another beautiful
    summer day.

June 2011

Heartstring's Farewell

Dawn awoke the silence from its deep solace
The strand of bygone quivering from the nightfall wind
Seeking connection for the soul's release comfort
To console yesterday's tears and broken embrace
A past has ended as daybreak starts to pave another path.

As the daylight begins to tie a birth of peaceful spirit
A new journey will open to surpass a nightfall
A starting point to hold each other's dream
A preface of boldness and strength binding to another hope
To end the dusk of past yet holding to what made it whole.

As the sun shines and rises to a fresh unknown
A renewed strand of life emerges in faith
The twine rebuilt to warm from a cold and painful slumber
To bid farewell and letting go of twilight's gloom
For yesterday is complete – from today shall bring tomorrow . . . the NEW
    DAY!

Good night, Papa
July 2011

I Do ...

Through the silhouette of my happy tears,
I've walked the aisle of an enchanted dream,
I see not the stars falling like a curtain of rain,
Rather a dusk of wish from anyone but me coming true
Today is my day . . . my very day with YOU.

The trees brushed each crisp leaves,
Reaching and swaying to a wind's song
Some falling and drifting through the season's call,
Outside I can see it changing to its mystic view,
Inviting creatures from their hovel solace,
Uniting and binding TWO souls in the skies.

From inside – I felt so delicate . . . so fragile
With the world holding me to its crest,
Tossing and turning, I started to sink within,
What is happening today, must it be true?
Recalling each scene, I smiled nonchalantly,
One by one . . . the scenes moved like a grand design,
Seem like a limitless clarity of a fairy tale somehow.

As the tick of every second come to pass,
I clasped a hand back to a world of childhood realms,
Slowly, my senses tickle . . . my thoughts quiver,
To the depths of a cluttered garden of the beautiful rose garden,
I started to laugh at the way he was speaking,
I have to pinch myself just to keep believing,
I traced his face with my eyes
Taking notes of his lips with that wonderful smile.

My senses continued to run wild,
Those intense eyes staring back with purity of life
Lips that gently moved in grace of sincerity
Words coming out like a silent prayer of a journey with a voice of comfort
Hand in hand strongly holds a bond of faith and trust
In each other's love, it feels safe and it fills a promise
For whatever comes . . . wherever it may lead US now or whenever . . .
Let it be my solemn vow . . . I DO!

Written for friends for their wedding day
Feb 2012

A Silent Journey

The sound of the alarm signalled a start
The clock ticked like humming bluebirds
Its melody echoed like a sweet ballad
I tossed and turned around only to trace a smile
I gazed at the loving stare of courage
I looked through a glare of soul with faith
From within – I saw a moment of calm and a safe solace
And for that moment of surrender – all I needed was to let go.

The stillness of the day as the sun unhurriedly rose to its grandeur
The gentle wind soothed my face with a promise of reverie
As the trees swayed and danced with the song of the breeze
I sensed protection as thoughts lingered with comfort
While in that state, I felt a tender embrace
From then – I realised that moment of strength and hope
For that moment – I know I am towards a journey of something worthwhile.

The journey to finding my purpose – I hope to achieve.
The adventure to living a dream – I aspire to be.
The discoveries of wonderful memories – I have lived through.
The creation of another treasure – I wish to cherish.
The voyage to set out not alone – but with a hand to steer beside me.
And from this crossing – I travel with blithe in my heart.
With a silent whisper of prayer – an unspoken love song carries us along.

Feb 2012

Night Lamp

I sat underneath the shades of trees – listening to its rhythm
The stillness of the night looks empty – it feels so serene
The blankness of the evening seem frightening and sombre
The void is creeping up my spine – it summons my worries
But as I gazed deeply into the clouds – the stars glistened strongly with pride
Carrying me to a place – another haven beneath the grandiose skies.

In my solitude I gave in completely to my imagination – a mind's eye to my
      senses
Into the darkness I walked without hesitation – rather in stubborn anticipation
In my pace I held on to a match – a symbol of courage to help on my way
I lighted a candle I call perseverance – to light my strength
As it flickers – a path of wisdom beckons my every step
As it glowed – a trail of hope charges me to keep moving.

With its brightness – I marvelled at the warmth it gave me
It shaved my determined soul – as the heat concealed me with inspiration
As I held the lamp closely with content – the dark shades became small
I saw a spark of a new promise – my guide to a journey unknown
The sight of it sent me to a beautiful awakening – of life's meaning
That after the dusk there is dawn – another breakthrough of tomorrow.

I opened my eyes to watch the setting sun from the horizon with a smile
The crickets awakened to its rest – chirping their joyous song
The frog joined in with its melody – a symphony of the evening
The cool breeze swiftly moves – as the sound features a beautiful hymn
As the gentle moon prepares to rise—
the sky blankets the dusk like a choir
And then the stars glistened to its regal – to happily light my way back
      home.

For Mama
Apr 2012

36

Moonlight Wishes

The sunlit bids farewell to rest making way to the evening's light
The calmness of the dark lures as the cold breeze filters the air
As the sun's array fade into space – the world looks subtle yet full of charm
Came a flash to brighten the sundown in soft caress
And glazing through the earth with a spell of enchantment.

As the twilight spread towards the horizon, stars peek and flicker glittering the
    clouds
The moon bloomed to full existence as stars twinkle and shine
Spreading radiance to guide the way through the dusky streets
Like a lighthouse it showers with the promise of fresh unfamiliarity
And gently gather dreams – creating hope to every wish to make.

Starry starry night, let me paint the rainbows throughout the skies
Silver grey clouds covering the world like sparkling eyes
I wish for happiness – filled with love of family and the people I meet
I wish for a good life – wrapped in strength to live each day
Moonlight, moon bright grant my wish I pray
That as I lay down to slumber deep, tomorrow will be okay
And it's another day to keep.
For Daldel, the Fighter.

Jan 2014

The Silver Moon Song

The evening skies
Wrote a song
To my heart for my soul
I'm in my thoughts of finding you
Of wanting you here with me.

My heart can't sleep
My soul too deep
In your eyes I'm looking tonight
I'm holding you in my arms
And missing you here with me.

The silver moon lights your smile
A trace of love in your eyes
My heart just beats
No words to speak
Only our souls collide.

A melody for you and me
A rhythm of love we danced
As we hold on tight
And I'm kissing you
Tenderly tonight.

The evening skies
Wrote a song
To my heart for my soul
My heart can't sleep
I'm in too deep
Wishing you here with me now.
Oh silver moon
Please hear my plea
I want my sweet knight with me.

Jan 2014

A Promise to Keep

Staring through a misty glass window – been raining for days . . . swirling
    down in spiral waves
I felt chills trembling down my spine – touching every limb, every fibre of my
    being
I start to feel numb – tears made my eyes cloudy
It felt so dark, made things so grey and gloomy – felt so alone.

I look so desolated – so wretched in the steady downpour of the rain
So timid from the over casted skies
So tiny that I want to bloat myself – I want to be seen in the rain as it fell in
    sheets
I want to shout so loud – that my cries may be heard and hoping the
    feeling may vanish along the way.

I started to view things in different perspective, picture life into the present
Here I am, I feel like living in a slow pace – feels easier that way, I thought.
Though there's so much to see – so much to do with all chances and
    options for me
For a somebody that I might become – somewhere that I might be.

Continued to trail on my thoughts, I stopped to smile
Something has reminded me to feel this way – light and peaceful
All the doubts – fear seem to have left me

In my heart, soon I will find what might be and could be a tomorrow.
Remembering the promises made – words of promise I'll always be keeping
Things being said that has kept me going until now
I don't know when , where and how it will come – a come what may
Yet, it has made me believe to live each day – something to look forward to
    without reserves.

But now why am I tempted to quit? – Why am I losing the courage?
My hold is starting to loosen its grip – My faith becoming hazy as the anchor
begins to rust and crease

The rock has starting to sink from where it's standing – crippling into shreds of
weakness.

Just then, with captive innocence I weighed everything in quiet solace – in
my own haven
Such peculiar experience – such false expression made me quiver
Strange features can be seen but I felt nothing – so numb
I only have a chance to restore what's left of me – what was instilled in me
over time.

I don't want to live in this hollow grounds – pointless and shallow
My whole system beamed and my grief lifted up and shattered in pieces of
glass
It's not the end of the world – I must go on and keep trying
A realisation burst in air – laid down is a blueprint of a new year to start.

There's no use in crying over spilt milk, they say
What can ease such rejection – is to bind my dreams somehow
Broken words are words that should be scrapped and forgotten
Deep inside I know I can still go on – for I am strong
In one's life there is hope – clasped within and reigns inside like a lion

Concede at every failure that weakness is but a strength of my making

With each blessing I am holding is a silhouette of my imperfections and the
scars of who I am
A matter of patience – faith becomes the centre and my mantelpiece
Perhaps in another time, wonderful promises will draw closer in time
By then it blossoms to life's beautiful surprises as each wish aligns in it's
sphere
I shall live with faith – a silent prayer and a promise to keep.

For Dadz, you said this is your favourite
Jan 2014

The Night Wing

Flying in an angel's wings, with a sparkle of fairy dust
Eyes widen as it glows with every thought – a silent wish
As the light flickers, it lit through a spot in my heart
It's brightness arrayed a fear of being alone
It stalked my doubts filling me with emptiness
Clutching a prayer and believing that wishes do come true.

As the sun began to set its course
Clouds round the place with a smile to greet one sign of moonlight
Crickets on choir as the moon entangles with the sun's brightness
Misty wind carefully blowing to a birth of every daffodils and carnations
Dewdrops fill the pine cones as the leaves of stood in courage
To fill each thought memories of my childhood – with happy thoughts.

As the night birds sing melodies of inspiration, I watched the violet skies
Street lamps lit the paths from strength to strength
Endless shadows of an oak tree echoes the night as it sways in grace
Carrying my heart to harmonic songs
As the hum of ballads soothes my loss – keeping my sanity
Distracting the night – a life away from you.

I looked straight to a fairy star, I see you with arms stretched out to cuddle
    my sorrows
As tears trickles and tall on my cheeks, I can feel your hand caressing my
    face with a promise
My shoulder starts to shrug with fear, I can see a smile – showing a thousand
    strength
That everything will be alright, as a voice whispers a promise to fill my
    emptiness
You and I, here are lying awake no matter the distance
You and I, here could be waking up tomorrow I know we are never far.

As I close my eyes tonight – my knight is there for me
As I sleep tonight – you will come to rescue me from my loneliness
As I dream tonight – you will cradle and hush me from my cries
Tonight as the stars sparkle – a light will guide your way safely back home
My raven who'll be flying deep into the clouds with persistence
My night wing to hold my every imperfections with gentleness until the
    morning's light.

Jan 2014

The Skyscraper

Look up . . .
See the vastness of the blue blanket
Gaze at the cotton clouds form
Search for the deep colour of peace
And wrap yourself around in velvet hue.

Look on . . .
The sun rises to its subtle peak
The birds flock to reach and seek
The wind blowing gently on your cheek
And lull yourself to slumber deep.

Look back . . .
How you felt when you start to fly
Felt the goose bumps gather by
Your heartbeat pulsating to a high
And your mind rushing through the mile.

Look forward . . .
Beneath that silver lining of your grief
Above lies a challenge may be steep
Beyond there awaits another hope, just believe
Because you belong to the sky, it is where you smile so meek!

Jan 2014

When It's Over

Say it . . .
In silence I stared vacantly in space – shocked at what I am hearing
I feel numb and calloused as my eyes starts to fill with tears
I am trying to shake off that feeling of disgust and betrayal
Of what you have just said – I can't believe you really said it.

When . . .
You said there's someone else – that you didn't mean it?
You said it just happened – that you just suddenly fell for her?
You said she's different – that you think she's the one for you?
But maybe you have forgotten – that's the same reason you said when you
    chose me?

It's over . . .
My heart felt like it is being torn into pieces – stabbed a number of times
My breathing seem to have stopped for a while each time you moved your
    lips as you speak
The sound of your voice seem broken – and my silence became a torture.
You turned your back and walked away – left me in the cold, winter rain.

Now it's over . . .
As the rain poured heavily – angry as the thunder roared in the horizon
I shouted – as slowly you faded away from the curtains of rain
"How dare you hurt me this way – you don't deserve me for I am more . . . I
    am far better."
I let out my emotions – cried as hard as I can along with each rainfall
I say it's over – you are nothing more to me but just a blur.

Feb 2014

Just a little more time ...

A little . . .
Let a teardrop fill the emptiness
Let me wonder how lonely must I've been
With all this pain in my heart
And the misery of my soul
I wish your gentle touch can fade them away
That my soul may be set free
From a shadow of fear . . . of doubts
From the clutches of hope
Of loving you.

More . . .
Frightened by your disguise
The promise you have once made
I thought will soon come
Tell me how will I survive?
Waiting for such terrible lies
How could you break my heart?
When nothing is left of me
Only the agony of regret.

Time . . .
You want another chance
To fulfil that dream . . . our dream?
You said you will make it up
You said "Sorry" for leaving me
That meant a lot because it matters to me
Much as I thought you will come back
But none of your stories are done
When I have given you the chance.

Just a little more time, I said
In time I will be whole again
Just a little more time, I asked
Until when will this hurting end?
Just a little more time, I wondered
When will this heartache end
When I know you will never return
Not now, nor tomorrow – it's over and never again!

Feb 2014

Lost Love

Laying down all alone – night feels cold and empty
Tossed and turned – restless and shivering like a frightened child
The rain pouring and muds thrashing from one corner to another
Gazing from my window – the clouds look like angry dragons blowing
   thunder and lightning.

The weather seem to guess my moods – tracing my veins protruding from
   my temple
Pulses racing – heart so heavy and ready to let go
Hints of denial – that I am crushed . . . that I am dying inside
Although I know I said I don't need you – but I do . . . I really do.

Tonight – I want to be alone but I can't and I don't want to
You've made me get used to having you around – the nights were never
   cold
I was always wrapped tenderly in your arms – locked tightly and safely
Holding me as endless and kissing me forever.

We laughed together – although our jokes were silly and corny
We both had dreams – made plans for the future
We've made promises – made a pact
We had our lives ready for tomorrow – but tomorrow is gone.

I trembled from the pain – my soul pierced by an arrow of misery
I closed my eyes not to be shaken from the memories of you
I want to shut you out – one who got away from my life
Losing you is a nightmare – and will haunt me for a while.

Forgetting you is hard – realising you are gone and have moved on is the
   hardest
Loving you was easy – being with you and having you beside me was the
   easiest
Losing you is losing myself – knowing from tonight I will be on my own
Healing will be a challenge – yet I am sure I will find myself again . . . in time.

Feb 2014

47

This Thing Called Love

LOVE, what's the perfect description can you fit in?
Is it a virtue of charity … an emotion … a miracle … a feeling?
Feelings of security … pleasure … happiness … or heartaches and
    miseries?

They say love has many secrets
Sects that can fill every corner, every space of the heart
Unfolds every emptiness that surrounds you
Banded to connect and unite as one.

Like the sun that glows to greet the morning's mist
That its brightness gives you a promise
A promise of hope and a new beginning
A new start and a fresh breath of air.

Like the moon that glimmers in the night
That lightens the shadows of darkness
Yielding every ardent pleas of the frightened heart
And becomes a shield from dusk 'til dawn.

Love endures, love conquers and gives meaning to a once senseless past
It gives magic to the once un-enchanted life
It tortures whenever it is left unsaid
And tingles your passion in every moment to cherish.

Love has reserves when hurt and in pain
It either leaves a lesson or marks a stain
Love has its own retribution and rewards
Love will reveal your secrets in any language of the heart.

Feb 2014

One Love Affair

The party is today?
Just saw the post-it reminder on the fridge
What am I going to wear?
I still have not decided yet, I think!
Panic stricken went back to my room
Scouring over my party dresses
Little red, blue, black dress? – choices no end.
Ah, the little black one and strappy stilettos never goes wrong.

Getting ready I feel like a pro
A touch of blush here, mascara there
And to top it all, my favourite red lipstick
Now I'm ready to paint the town red hot
Hop on the taxi – my carriage awaits
Like a chauffeur driven car for a lady with flare
As we drove off the Saturday streets
I can't help but whisper a prayer of finding a love affair.

Arriving I am excitedly greeted at the doorway
Welcoming glass of sparkling wine to flush the hint of shyness
Out in a crowded space the room feels smaller
Out in the corner of my eye another pair stares intently
I turned to find out who but was caught in surprise
The owner of those piercing look is right in front
There's that mischievous smile that can melt hearts
And that manly voice that can weaken the knees.

He introduced himself and asked for a dance
I gave him my name as we walked towards the dance floor
The music's enchanting as we slow danced
Our bodies moved in every motion of the notes
We talked so little as the song filled our thoughts
Seemed like we are talking in silence
Our minds sending messages in codes.

The music is over, the dance is complete
We found ourselves out in the patio
We talked and talked under the moon lit skies
The stars burning the surface like crystal chandeliers
The place looks secluded as the party has ended
The nightfall is over – a break of dawn has come
Both in one accord got up to leave and thanked the hosts.

Walking along the streets the lamp posts bowed in grace
You held my hand – our fingers entwined
The breeze brushed my face sending chills to my spine
You wrapped your arm around my shoulders as I rest my head on yours
The warmth of your embrace lifting me high
It feels like magic as we stroll the path
For together we have found a love affair to last.

For Ru
Feb 2014

A Love Story

Hurriedly towards the train station
I must catch the next train
Walking in strides
Got my train ticket
It fell from my pocket
As I picked it up
Another hand touches mine.

I looked up
You looked down
I smiled
You smiled back
I said thank you
You said it's okay
Then you walked away towards the exit.

Slipped in towards the platform
I can't help but smile
I run my fingers through my hair
I felt my face warm and blushing
I thought your eyes was beautiful
I thought your smile was lovely
But I didn't get your name.

I kept staring blankly at nowhere
My thoughts wandering about you
My mind racing to wondering who you are
Your hand touching mine was electric
I felt a thud of my heart like a drum beat
I felt goose bumps at the back of my neck
Mr. Nice guy has gone by.

Train stopped in front of me
People getting off passing my way
I let them through before hopping in
Then settled in a seat as thoughts rushing my mind
I snapped back to reality
When I felt a stare so familiar
A look piercing through mine

I looked up and you looked down
I smiled and said "Hi"
You smiled back and said "Hello"
You stretched your hand to shake mine
I held your hand and you held mine
That was the beginning of a love story
Of how we have become entwined.

Feb 2014

A Gift of Love

Walking around the city mall all day
Have been going from one shop to another
Searching for that special gift
Valentine's Day is Friday and still can't decide on a gift
Sure a card will do, I guess but really?
I swear if I don't get a gift in the next shop, I muttered
Kept scolding myself for doing this last minute
And suddenly something caught my eye
Oh, there you are – found at last!

I hurriedly went inside the store, almost closing time!
Whilst looking inside the glass cabinet – I felt a little disappointed – I can't
    touch it then and there
The lady at the store approached me with a smile, " May I help you?"
I replied with a hint of excitement, "Yes please!"
She opened the cabinet and handed me the item
I felt like a child buying a toy for the first time.
Without a blink I whispered, "Finally!"

At the counter, the lady told me it's the last of the two items.
I asked why only two and she replied, "Well, it's two of a kind gift."
She then guided me to the door ready to close – being the last customer
Curiosity struck me – "Who bought the other kind?", I wondered
On my way home, I thought of you and smiled.
I felt so proud of myself for finding this gift
I thought of the other kind – then wished whoever gets it will feel so special.

In my head I played a scene – what wrapper to use
Where to put the gift so you can easily spot it
Words to write on the card – of what I truly feel
I imagine you finding your gift as I purposely left it before going to work
I imagine your face lighting up reading the card
I imagine you opening the box and taking the gift out.
I imagine what you would say and how your voice would sound like
Most of all, I imagine you holding the gift – a gift of love everlasting.

Valentine's Day
Feb 2014

The Two of a Kind
(A Gift of Love)

Friday, 14 February Valentine's Day
Finally, I can't wait to give you your gift
As planned, I left it on the coffee table hoping you'll find it
Tiptoeing, walked to the door so not to wake you up
Left a little earlier than usual so I can leave work early
We have decided to have dinner for two at home
As I am the chef, I am in charge of the menu
As you know your wine, you will be choosing our drink – white, red, rose.

The day seem to drag as I await for your call
Time slipping gently – I want to wind it to move faster
Tic toc – I hear it tic in my head as the toc tortures my existence
Can't help myself from staring at my phone – waiting
Impatient – I am tempted to call you, maybe
Then hesitated – telling myself to wait for a little bit longer
I need some distractions – do something else other than think of you
Waiting can be ruthless when you are expecting something.

I decided to do some work to kick you out of my mind for the meantime
Work became busy – hectic schedules all day
Then I remembered – need to check for any messages
Surprised to realise – "No messages?"
I felt a stabbing pain in my heart – "Didn't like my gift?"
I felt hurt and betrayed – "Maybe there's someone else?"
I want to cry and shout as I stared vacantly into nowhere
I started telling myself – "I am sure I will get an answer later on. After all this?"

Going home is hard, I can't move and scene is starting to play
I imagined different pictures – looked at different angles
Turning the door key is heavy – it feels like a movie in slow motion
As I opened the door, there you are with that smile melting me away
In your hand – you held your gift and then I became speechless
The other piece – you are holding the other piece of the puzzle!
I run and hugged you so tight crying – had to ask me to let go so you can
     breathe
That's when I remembered the lady saying – "it's special two of a kind" . . .
     you and I are the two of a kind my Sweet Valentine!

Valentine's Day
Feb 2014

Happy Thoughts of Saturday

Just sitting at the edge of my bed, in my solitude uninterrupted
Within the four corners of my room, staring down the feet
I am in my own y space, I call my solace and my haven
The stillness of the moment, I start collecting my thoughts
The silence prodding my soul into deep and innate.

I closed my eyes to hear the sound of air as I inhale
The tranquil motion of my every breath I take is sedating
The rhythm of my heart slowly lulls my being like a symphony
The pulse beating into a melody of something wonderful
Into a song, I am humming happy thoughts.

As the morning's rays warm my face through the window
Outside I hear the buzz of children playing in the streets in their bikes and
    trikes
While grandmas shout in worry little ones might fall off their bikes
Moms peering from the kitchen window with flour on her face baking
    cookies
Dads washing their cars and playing ball with older sons

Can you remember your childhood weekends when school is over?

When the week's hard work is finished and done
The time to throw ball with dad you look forward and not to be missed
The time for baking cakes and cookies with mom and grandma too
These are the happy days on happy wonders of Saturday fun.

Feb 2014

Drifted Pain

Sometimes things come when least expected – a surprise and a blessing
When wishes just pop out from nowhere – from the closet of dreams
Thoughts that seem hard to understand – difficult to comprehend
A mind full of mysteries – vivid to the imagination
A spectrum of sights – so full to a timid heart and a broken spirit.

Recognising each detail can be startling – striking the innermost being
Describing every feeling – it leaves so much questions and uncertainties
Void of the answers – of what to expect and what to find
There is a limit – of what I can take and how to bear it all again
But there are chances – to outgrow the hurt and get rid of the unwanted.

Often unaware of the forces – the shield I created in my life
A strength gathers my lost spirit – that somehow I can get out of the pitfalls
Hope shows up – to cradle and embrace me to safe haven
Faith displays to the horizon – to drift away each pain and memories
So life comes after to start anew – putting me back to pieces and be able
    love to again.

Mar 2014

Loving You

My world whirling in the four corners of my bed
Tossed and turned on my crumpled sheets
I closed my eyes – my mind shut from the outside world
I took a deep breath – to feel the thumping of my heart
In silence – counted the beat of my pulse
As I opened my eyes – your face I see in my mind.

Is this love? – I wondered with the image of you in my thoughts
I traced the shade of your face – your eyes telling me something
With a brush of my imagination – I broke into fragments
As the figure resembled a beauty – so unique
The story is entrancing – it captured every fabric of my being
A music that touched my soul – taking me captive.

In the midst of my illusions – I walked in shambles
As your apparition sent me speechless – your smile held me motionless
Gazing through your eyes – you stared back into the depth of me
As your lips moved – barely understanding what you're saying
I am left paralysed – a magnet pulling me to you
Mesmerising my sanity – an obsession to be with you.

I shifted to the side of the bed – snapping myself out of this fantasy
The ray of the sun sparked my senses back into reality
A shadow slowly walked towards me – my comprehension awakened
A soft whisper in my ear tickled – I giggled to every word
I stretched my arms out – to cuddle me safely in your embrace
My heart in longing – loving you loving me and an ever after.

Mar 2014

But Never Love

The lights are flickering walking along the quiet road
The moon watching over with its brightness – a hope to every prayer
Stars continue to glitter over distant skies
Waiting to fall to every ardent wish – every whisper of plea
As the clouds wrap the world like a safe blanket
A spell of enchantment encapsulates the night
To fill it with magic – a night to seize this very moment.

The wind blows softly like a ball of cotton
The breeze brushing my skin gently as I shiver from my thoughts
The glint of each star peering through the massive skies
The shadows of the trees swaying as its branches stretches out
I pulled my jumper as the cold night sends chill down my body
I sighed, never thought that being alone can take its toll
In surrender, a tear starts to fall – its warmth short-lived.

Such moment like this, emptiness fills me
The seconds of every minute seeping every turn of time
Another sigh came – hugged myself in the hope to protect my emotions
As the grey clouds cover the moon from its resting place
The stillness felt serene – embracing me to safety
It sensed what I'm thinking – my deep thoughts laid out
Filling my heart with greater expectations of what tomorrow brings.

The wind continued to chime through the night's solitude
The sound imitating the beat of my heart – a solemn rhythm
My thoughts wandered – questioning my feelings
"Am I doing the right thing – is it worth it . . . are you worth it?"
I struggled with my emotions, I am confused about the answers – uncertain
    of what I really want
My mind gave me a reason – "But never love, it only ends in heartache!"
But then again my heart answered – "Loving you is a risk I'm willing to take."

Mar 2014

Intoxicated

So many questions – doubts and fears clouding her mind
The why's and the how's creeping inside – it makes no sense at all
The what's and the where's – blocking every thoughts blurring her sanity
The could it be's and the maybe's – wavering like the seas crushing every
    sand castles delicately made
And the but's and yet's echoes – like a whirl of a storm along the toxic
    waters.

The journey taken isn't straight and narrow
The path? – Walking is like an uphill battle and the climb so steep
The tunnel seem endless and tiring – the light is too far ahead
Each step is heavy – her feet feels like being dragged in chains
With every move she feels nauseated – intoxicated as her blood runs
    through every part of her.

Asking all the questions – there she finds a glimmer of hope peeking
Putting all the answers – there she finds her faith along the way
Taking the journey – there she finds her unmarked courage soaring
Gathering all the strength – there she finds her spirit set free
And finding her soul – she discovered real love and living.

In her eyes – I see pain behind every smile
In her smile – I sense loneliness and the whispered prayer
In her prayers – I hear her silent cries and ardent wishes
In her wishes and every tear – I can feel true strength and real courage
And in that strength . . . in her courage – there I have found a pure heart
    showing love like no other.

For Daldel, let's keep fighting

Mar 2014

On Broken Wings

Gazing through tainted shadows of the searing clouds
My mind swirling. Spins to travel to distant shores
Soaring through narrow spaces of time in my solitude in this realm
My soul touching a promise to a nowhere
Of how to reach the place I have always dream to exist – to live loving and
to love living!

In my emptiness I've searched – met mountains of challenge
Here in front of me (right now) are hills of doubts . . . valleys of fears towering
over my diminished strength for I am not sure if I can hold on
Passing through roads of weakness echoes along my sunken emotions
I seem to be walking through a tunnel of sorrows in curves and hoops
I felt like crossing through a sea of tears stumbling through rocks – in pain
and seeing you in pain.

In every travel – it feels like I am lost and in circles trying to find my way
home
I wandered through moments and glimpse of hope as I gaze the horizon
. . . there is a beginning
That the journey . . . your journey continues across thousands of wishes to
glimmer on.
There are signs everywhere to carry and redirect through pocketful of
courage
So in your flight – fate will shine and destiny lives on a purpose.

As I take each breath, I look at you – a sigh deep within my thoughts
There's a direction – a hidden strength found within you
In my heart – a light I see . . . as my soul eases in calming hue
In my mind I understood living – my spirit soared beyond the clouds
There is an existence – a realism to live upon the vastness of the skies.

Contemplating with life I saw a sparrow arching its wings with great pride
Looked through its eyes I tried searching through its thoughts
Peering through I have sensed courage – I have read a mind full of wisdom
It gave a view that for even a down casted spirit – in my weakened psyche
A sparrow's eyes – pierced my soul with a gracious strength of hope to
    believe – in living!

With every direction I glided with my instinct – collided with my courage
In all aspects – I wondered for reasons but have never found some answers
Somehow I know there will always be another way – somewhere to find my
    answers
That to some place – I believe you will find a rebirth – renew dreams for
    every moment and every waking time
For even on broken wings, though on splinted arms – I know you will keep
    holding on
Entwined with a bond of faith – protected with a love so pure – on broken
    wings you shall fly and soar again!

Mar 2014

Falling

I never imagined how it is to fall in love so deeply
Just then out of nowhere I met you – a creature of uniqueness
I thought of perfection – though you may be filled with defects
I describe you with elegance – though you may be wrapped with dullness
I imagine you with refinement – though you may be clothed with roughness
I believe you are a handful of goodness – though you may have a tough
    exterior.

Falling – your coming has taken me aback
Falling – was something I did not expect
Falling – my mind had so many reasons to hesitate and fear of being hurt
Falling – my heart had so much more reasons to take risks
Falling – made me realise that falling for you is meant to be
Falling – is finding myself how to dream and hope again
Falling – is believing love is to live my life again.

With you falling is not a worry – you are there to catch me
With you fear is nothing – you are there with courage to keep me safe
With you I don't think of losing – you are there within reach
With you hoping is sharing – as your faith stands firmly on the ground
With you everything seems fine – you made sure it's going to be okay
With your tender touch – I can't find enough reason not to need you
With a thoughtful gaze – I can't deny learning to love you more.

Each moment with you is a garden of Eden – like a paradise island
Each time of weakness – you are an arm of strength
Each day of pain – you relieve me with a pocketful of hope
Each dream we make – your promise is of good intentions
When tears fall at a moment of sadness – you wipe it with caress
At a chance of happy thoughts – you shine with a smile full of life
For each emptiness I feel is covered with surprises – beautiful moments to
    cherish with you.

April 2014

The Clay Master

In a slow pace I searched for a path – to guide me through
Signs I see is wrapped in stripes of enquiry – a scheme to cover the way
Each symbol designed with mazes and puzzles to solve
Mysteries bonded – to use logic rather than guess
To analyse with reasons – a balance for making decisions
To weigh each challenge – with a hope to keep going
To comprehend with a stable mind – for a leap of faith to try harder
And a gentle listen to my heart – to find a right choice in life.

I closed my eyes – it feels dark without a hand to show directions
Passion stirring my senses – as my feet joined the ground
Doubts clinging – as suspicions clog my thoughts
A moment of weakness and of loss – frightened to what is ahead
Finding answers I realised takes so much of me – my faith and my will
    almost empty
The journey is far ahead – the road endless and winding
The walk is heavy – my body fighting to stay sturdy to every step
My strength is consumed – body and mind slowly draining away.

I thought of giving up – but perseverance is pushing me
I thought of turning back – but my motivation is prodding me
I thought of finding the easier way – but curiosity is prompting me
But then I kept going – there are signs of courage showing me everywhere
I see trees of wisdom – coaching me to stand on my ground
I smell wild flowers of purity – coaxing my heart to cast away doubts
I felt the breeze of hope – enticing my mind to believe in my spirit
The beauty of each senses – carrying my soul to my dreams.

Through this I have recognised – my life is my purpose
I stand contented and serene – the world is my garden as I am the clay
    master
Everything is mine to mould – to be what I want it to be
That every soil I gather – there is a chance to find an art of nature
That every source around me – is a choice to create my own design
To find myself among others – even in my imperfections
To find happiness and peace – even in a world of madness
And to find innocence and simplicity – even in a life of contemporaries.

April 2014

Incomplete

The day you said you have to go – that it is time to say goodbye
That day my world shattered – I felt like broken into fragments
I did not show how dejected I've felt – I just couldn't
I have to show them that I am strong – I have to for you
I need to make sure things are taken care of – being selfish is the last thing
You have asked for me to lead – be the one to show them the way
If you only knew – that day was the moment I felt imperfect and
    incomplete.

I grew up always having you around – my rock and my solid ground
You always had the answers to my questions – about life, of living and to
    dream
You always had that gentle voice to soothe me – whenever I am down and
    heartbroken
You never struggled to find words – whenever I am lost and miserable
You never failed to teach us – to keep the faith, to believe and always hope
You have never been away without us – our adventures together was never
    dull
You and us – the perfect puzzle . . . a flawless maze now unfinished and
    incomplete.

Today should be a day to celebrate – a remembrance of your remarkable
    life
Been so long since I saw your smile – so meek yet so cheeky
Been awhile since I heard you laugh – it was an infectious giggle
Been sometime since I last listened to your playful stories – all made up but
    full of fun
Been years if I start counting since I sang along with you – playing the
    ukulele was a bonus
Been ages since I went to sleep to your lullabies – the gentle stroke of the
    hair was special
Today, for moments like this – just thinking of you I am still lost and
    incomplete.

For Abuela
April 2014

Faded Photographs

Staring at old memories – reminiscence of a history
Images of places visited – beautiful landscapes recreated
Sketches of faces – a tell-tale story of every moment
Drawings of expressions – a standstill of emotions
Painting a portrait that matches a thousand words
A motion picture that revives a feature of life's yesterday
Details and profiles of who we are and what we have become.

The old photographs sent me back to memories almost forgotten
The images of smiles and poses brought excitement like it just happened
The places in the background reminded me of the stories in an instant
Moments of what we used to talk – the conversations of dreams and
    aspirations
The expressions of each figure traces true feelings
Emotions wielded – a masquerade behind the realities of life
A sense of susceptibility – feelings and thoughts of what was then and now.

From each piece describes a portrayal – a mirror of my experiences
I sensed a narration – recalled the beautiful anecdotes and humorous
    remarks
Certain impressions of the unexpected – candid shots of the passing
Features of a mood – a laugh, a smile, an act to evoke the plot
As I turned every page of the album a novel is imagined – a soundtrack in
    rhythm
The art of faded photographs – are views of my past and treasures in a box
The recollections of my existence – the memoirs of life to keep.

April 2014

The Hourglass

Words come in tiny bits – like shattered pieces and puzzles
A little of this . . . more of that and some of it
When put together shows a meaning – printed in different shades and
   shapes
When read – it conjures an explicit remark
As it is spoken – commands a language of feelings
As each sound lists a dozen signs – a symbol of emotion
Maybe love . . . maybe life . . . maybe can be anything.

Looking through an hourglass – in a tube of time
Slowly the sand glides towards a tunnel of life
I see myself through it – silently sliding with every loose grain
As each piece falls with cautions of fear – giving up a dream
A frail hope appears – as blankness evaluates my timid mind
With a pile of regret from past mistakes – emotions mix with my fading
   strength
And with just a bottle of courage – I redirected my steps to taking chances.

Facing my fate serendipity found me – it touched my sense of longing
For knowing life is created with a purpose – it gave me a reason
For having a reason – a tainted glass melts into grace
As it clears away my doubts . . . my fears – my heart shifts to an awakening
As my mind sought resignation – my soul invites trust
At that point in time I know – my heart starts to see another dream
And that moment I realised- my dream of finding love is for me to turn the
   hourglass.

The hourglass spins the opposite – altering a faded picture into hue
As each grain of sand passes through – a story is written
Every word and every thought consumes the heart
Every beat of the heart connects – glides along a journey
The journey may not be straight – there will be clusters in each step
As the lump moves it eases through – a breath to take away
As time goes by we hold the key – to turn the hourglass of loving all over
again.

April 2014

The Canvas

Staring curiously at a blank wall – with questions in mind
It looks so vacant – unspoiled from tarnish and dirt
The plainness of it seem tamed – there is a sense of modesty yet cautious
The surrealist of it is uncompromising – innocent and naive
Evoking my imagination – to craft my emotions.

Viewing the spotless wall – I find my own self
An empty canvas set to be painted on – a life's creation
I started to fill my thoughts with memories – of faded photographs and the
    gallery of images
My emotions stitching together – figuring out a sketch
The brush strokes slowly weaving from one end to another – an abstract is
    formed.

As the painting slowly comes to life – it features a different scene
Illusions from a distance in a stereoscopic view – a perception of what I
    want to see
I took a step back – to reflect on what I have created
I started to realise – This is definitely not me!
What I am seeing is the replica of what I wish I am and what I thought I
    should be.

I reached deeper to my thoughts – my inner sensibilities
Who am I? What am I – what I have become?
Re-touching the prints – I have found the beauty of my being
Free-handed and guided with the true essence of life's art – I have found
    love
Now I am staring intently at the masterpiece – there I saw strength and a
    beautiful soul.

May 2014

Colours of Life

Life has many colours – different meanings in different angles
Life at times is difficult to understand – difficult to reach and makes us
    wonder
But looking outside in we accept – life can be a rainbow of dreams
It teaches us lessons – make us realise its beauty
It makes us glow – to whatever darkness we may be in
It makes us grow – to finding our strength when we thought we have lost.

White – emptiness and fragile – a devoid of extreme highs or lows
Life living in stillness – a quiet calm and a vacant spot of silence
A pause for time – to surface when needed
A chance for change – an unmasking of mood
A slow moving of one's state of mind.

Black – is darkness like a sombre in hue
A passion gone – cold and calculating
A struggle of faith for a bleak of hope – a shadow of notion
A blemish of perfection in life – desolate of emotions
A feeling of fear and a battle of doubts inside.

Yellow and Gold – some call it jealousy
I call it a new day – a new horizon
The sun has risen – a new hope has arrived
It sends waves of passion – a renewal of accepting new challenges
Filled with new defences – a rage for living life.

Green – The earths unripen sphere
The trees are its warriors to guard nature's offspring
As the leaves changes every season
Its roots have claimed the land
And the grass blankets the world – to keep us grounded.

Blue – clear skies and deep settled seas
A peaceful resemblance of a blank canvas
A transparent crisp iced water – refreshing and tranquil
A tune of freedom – a serene blend of enchantment
It is the silence of the psyche – an unperturbed distance of the mind.

Red – the colour of blood flowing deep
A source of energy and emotions
A palpating sound of our every depth
In every beat sends impulses to our thoughts – the desires of the heart
In a momentum – there is that sense of warmth within our soul.

Life is not always easy – its a profound depth of living
It is a continuous process – of aiming, losing and winning
It is a constant battle of wants and needs – of hopes and dreams
Life in the end is our blank paper – to design and create
And our life becomes our masterpiece – a priceless possession.

May 2014

A Shadow's Face

In my darkened room – I see a faint shadow lurking
Its move is delicate yet there is that cunning step
I shut my eyes so I may not see – my sight may be deceiving me
I imagined a plot of terror – my thoughts beginning to scare me
I can feel goose bumps – a chill in the air on a gloomy, rainy night.

My heart started to beat faster – like a beat of a drum
I can feel my breath racing – like I'm running away somewhere
Streaks of sweat collected on my forehead – slowly dripping down my face
I opened my eyes – frightened as I stared blankly on the ceiling
With a sigh of relief I relaxed and told myself – it's just my illusion.

I decided to keep the lights off – and thought of writing in my head
I started creating a scene of light – with mysteries and magic
I drew images of contentment – a sight that pleases the heart and soul
While this picture comes to life – I find myself gazing at a figure in the mirror
There's that shadow I see – a blank face staring back with eyes piercing
    through me.

I turned the lamp on – the subtle light welcoming the dark
The glow starts to comfort me – with a cheerful grin
Yet there is still that shadow prowling in wait
The shadow that's a make believe – a vision I conceived
Only then to realise the shadow was my reflection – reminding me to be
    spirit free.

May 2014

Out of Love

I left home this morning – with tears in my eyes
I sensed that things have changed – there's distance between us
It felt like we are strangers – a once bonded soul
It seemed like we are here now – but our mind is somewhere
Have we fallen apart – are our hearts taken?

The thought of it all – I find myself questioning
Have I done something – am I being unreasonable?
Have you done something – are you looking for someone else?
Am I expecting so much of you – when I should just lay low?
Or do you suppose to believe – I am no longer the one?

Tonight I came home – with hope in my heart
That maybe there is a reason – why we became so restrained
That maybe there is that time – when we feel we need space
Maybe there is that thought – building a space can be lonely and cold
Or maybe, just maybe as strangers – out of love we can fall again.

May 2014

As Time Goes By

With every tick of the clock – time is passing
Time is slowly moving to another pace – it is bound to end
As time goes by, starting means to begin unfolding pain and hurt
Every broken glass – the shattered pieces clutched
Banded to make it whole – scarred yet determined to face any challenge.
Although fragile – each mark is a piece of sanity.

As time goes by, every road taken may be tough to pursue
There may be struggles along the way – face another ordeal
Despite many gloomy consequences – there is that sense of resilience
A reason to fight – to change perceptions of failure
To change for the better – to find good in a bad situation
That even in hostility – in time all will be subdued.

As time goes by, yesterday will become a distant memory
Time in itself will become a past – a vision of bygones
The past will become a solitude of time – a sign of nothingness
Nothingness will only be a blank canvas – a chance to change
The canvas can become a plan – to find another vision and dream
Another spectre – to draw the blueprint of a new life.

As time goes by, life will seize to breath yet there will be another birth
There will be another creation – another masterpiece made
There will be a chapter written – another story to tell
There will be a place built – designed to its expectations
As time passes by, each piece will fade and may be repainted
For time just keeps going, until we realise when to let go and hold on to
    what keeps us alive.

May 2014

Once upon

Once upon a blue moonlight
I stowed away my shattered heart
Locked every drop of tears and shot of pain into a box
Threw away the key with a hope that maybe it will be found
To unlock the box and put the pieces of my heart.

Once upon a beautiful sunrise
I am bewitched by its glory and strength
The golden light bathing my soul with faith
And every ray of sun I see – there is a life and a reason to living
That every wish I make – believing in chances to take.

Once upon an orange sunset
I see not just hope but another dream and another song
As the evening slowly comes to an end I patiently await
For tonight as the stars light up the skies – in my silent whispers
There is tomorrow – a day to make moments to live by.

Once upon another moonlight
That yesterday's dream – my heart will soon find love
There is that certain someone with a lost key to unlock the box
The once broken pieces will be put back and made whole
Held with a promise to bind our hearts as one soul.

June 2014

Love is to Forever

There are a hundred things I imagine – like serendipity
A hundred more reasons why I keep dreaming a dream
A hundred times over to wish upon a star
And another hundred to hope that there will be a day
For hundreds and hundreds of thoughts I will find you one day.

There are a thousand moments I can think of – each happy moments
A thousand more of laughter – of silly things we do
A thousand times over to dreams – the plans we make together
And another thousand to fill our life with memories – in any kind of weather
For thousands and thousands of keepsakes – I treasure it with you.

There are a million stories to write – on our journey together
A million more are added – pictures to cherish and fill us
A million times over for trust and a promise – the life we choose
And another million to courage – a rock to every fall
For millions and millions to lifetime – love is forever, you and I.

Jul 2014

Today's just another morning

The alarm went off and there goes the snooze button
Give me five minutes, I said
Just five minutes to gather my thoughts
Another alarm? I asked
Can I have another five minutes more?
It is not just to gather my thoughts, I reasoned
It is now about my point of view.

I've decided to get up and organise myself for the day
Thoughts swirling and brainwaves in numerous things
A checklist of errands and my mission for today
A quest to complete, a challenge to accomplish
With a leap of faith that today will end with a smile
With a hope that this day will be something worth the while
To make it through until the sunset comes.

The sun beams have spread with grace
Walking along the streets I see the buzz of the day's beginning
Time to pick up the pace, a rushing hour
Buses and cars to and fro, travelling from here and there
Traces of smiles that greets you, while other's frowns you wish you didn't see
The same ordinary day, a commonplace we're contend with
Just another morning and another day
until tomorrow again.

Jul 2014

It's 2 AM

It's 2 am – the night's over as dawn and cold wind fills the air
I'm still wide awake – feeling chilly under the sheets
I pulled the blanket tighter to hopefully cover the draft
I tossed and turned to find a perfect pose to sleep
No matter how I try the bed still feels hollow and empty.

It's 2 am – my eyes still searching for a way
The void I feel inside is exhausting me – it's frustrating
There's this anxious feeling of waiting for tomorrow to come
I clutched the pillow next to me as I looked at the vacant spot
Running my hand on your crumpled space thinking how much I miss you.

It's 2 am – I stared at my phone wishing you've read my mind
There is that silent prayer – that maybe you woke up thinking of me
There is that whispered hope – that maybe you're missing me
There is that spark of warmth – that you dreamt of me
Just a "Hello" will be enough for me to shut my eyes.

It's 2 am – I decided to try as I am getting jaded
Then suddenly I hear a ring – I've got a message
I felt butterflies in my stomach – a sweet tingling in my ear
Excitedly I checked – a note from you saying, "Hush little one and close your
    eyes, I'm here."
It's 3 am – tightly I cuddled your pillow, now I'm off to beautiful slumber
    deep.

Aug 2014

Is Summer Over?

The ray of the sun is striking – my eyes are hurting as it warms my face
Maybe because I'm sat right at the sun's heat
I tried to use my hand to shield me – it gave a little relief
But I got tired from holding my arm up – I'm just tired altogether
But it doesn't matter now – the sun will be down soon.

I've been up all night – now it's the morning after
I've waited for you – you said you'll be home soon yet you're not
I could not sleep without you beside me – I got used to having you next to
    me
Spent the whole night counting the stars as it falls
But then it doesn't matter now – the sun will set soon.

Tears started to fall all over again – I can't understand why
When you left you just said, "I'll see you tonight."
Tonight became morning – you were a no show
I kept searching for reasons – I reached for answers
But it doesn't matter – the sun will be gone soon.

I sobbed at the thought of us – summer was great
We made promises to each other – made plans for tomorrow
Recounting our moments together – I realised summer was different
I kept to my illusions – to stop myself from hurting
But it doesn't matter now – the sun is slowly descending soon.

I wiped my tears away – trying to face reality
You are never coming back – you have traded me, you chose her
The lies and deceit – are obvious reasons why you run away
For one last time – I watched the sun set from afar to say "Goodbye"
And it doesn't matter now – the sun will rise tomorrow and so will I.

Aug 2014

Some Stupid Love Song

A one rainy Monday morning and the coldness is calming
With a cup of coffee on hand to warm my fingers
The place looks so quiet – it feels like I'm somewhere in space
I turned the radio on and the music filled the empty house
I sat on the lounge – feeling lazy, cosy and content
Yet something is missing – a certain someone isn't here.

As I finished my coffee then a familiar song is played
I tapped my finger on the cup to join the beat
I closed my eyes – the melody filled my mind as I sang along
In my thoughts I slowly painted a face – a familiar smirk I love seeing
Your image came in view – chanting the lyrics of the song with me.

As the music continues to play – you stretched your arms out
I reached to hold your hand – we danced like crazy even with four left feet
We giggled at each other's misery – you kept stepping on my toes as I do
    the same
We laughed and twirled like kids spirited away
Then we slow danced – all I hear are our hearts beat like a drum.

The music halted into a finish – another song came to play
You held me tight as my head rests on your shoulder – we moved to the
    rhythm
You raised my head – I looked up then you said, "I guess this is our new
    song."
I smiled back – I rest my head on your chest I whispered, "Yeah, some love
    song perfect for our crazy love."
I opened my eyes to reality – there you are sheepishly telling me, "I so crazy
    love you, Stupid."

Aug 2014

Because when ...

Because when . . .
You look at me I have shivers in my spine
Your eyes say the words I really want to find
As I look back, I can see your soul reaching out
A moment I feel your heart beating together with mine.

Because when . . .
You smile it melts my doubts away
It tells me a real story of your hopes and your life
As you utter words "I love you" tells me how much you do
I hear your promise of tomorrow and a life with you.

Because when . . .
Your embrace confines my fears and lock me to a secure place
In your arms I am safe – it is where I feel a reason to trust
As we hold each other's hand for hours we never let go
Together we make a journey wherever it takes us.

Because when . . .
I'm missing you, I think of you in every way
A puzzle solved, and souls bound to meet
Our imperfections make us just as perfect
A beautiful picture and a dream of an ever after.

Aug 2014

Just Maybe

Just maybe . . .
I am no longer that someone
Not that special you go crazy about
Not the same person you like to spend time with
Just maybe, I guess.

Just maybe . . .
I am too much to contend with
Too much to live with as the days passes by
Too much to listen to with so little to talk about
Just maybe, I thought.

Just maybe . . .
You have other things important than I
Other things to come first as I am now the last
Other people to speak to and places you rather be
Just maybe, I'm lost.

Just maybe . . .
I am too emotional that I am unreasonable
Feelings stirring my mind to be irrational
Feelings creating doubts to be dejected
Just maybe, I feel alone.

Aug 2014

Wishing

So many things I want to say
Emotions in my heart wrapped together
Thoughts in my head in line ready in time
And words in my mouth formed in unison
But there is no one here besides myself
So here, I'm wishing.

There are things I want to do
Pieces of puzzles to put together
My hands are ready to lay them out
My brain all set to solve each part
My eyes all clear to see it complete
Yet here, I'm wishing.

A lot of things I want to see
A list written with a smiley face
A tick box on the side to go through as I go along
Excitement engulfing my thoughts
That these will be something I wanted
But still, I'm wishing.

All the places I want to go
Somewhere I want to just sit back and relax
A nook where I can gather thoughts
A corner to find inspiration and discoveries
As my mind maps each passing hour
Here I am, finding.

Aug 2014

Friday …

Feeling exhausted from the days that don't seem to end
From the beginning of work week there goes the endless task
From when I start there is that hope for a good week
From that moment there is that notion of counting hours and soon counting
   days.

Reeling over the days as it slowly passes by
Rain or shine the weather just comes to capture its purpose
Restless nights becomes a thing of the past
Relieved and relaxed to completing the list of errands at hand.

In so many ways I start to make my plans
I imagine how I will be spending my time off – away from it all
I picture myself in a hammock between palm trees swaying to the breeze
I can see the waves rushing and touching the sand as the sound fills the air.

Danced in the moonlight as the stars flicker like diamond lights
Dancing bare feet as my feet feel the soft sand that tickles my toes
Dusk 'til dawn nature's sound will be chanting like a lullaby
Day rises to its fullest and shines to another magical play.

As I fill my hours with these happy thoughts
Another hour is completed, another minute fulfilled
As I hear the clock ticking in motion, every second is moving on
Another moment of excitement draws me nearer to going home.

Yet today may be just a thought that crossed my mind
Yesterday's bad day is just another day gone
Yearning to fill my days with beautiful scenes and places
Yes today is almost over and tomorrow is mine to take away as it comes.

Sep 2014

Seems like a Fairy Tale ...

Scanning through the pages deciding on which meal to order
The picture looks so appetizing and is enticing my palate
It made my mouth water and so as my stomach complaining of hunger
The smell of the aroma inside the place is captivating, I thought
The buzzing sounds in the room felt lyrical as each one catches up to the
days' end.

While I browse through the menu, I felt a tingling sensation – sent shivers to
my spine
A pair of eyes intently gazes through the laminated brochure
I giggled like a little girl covering my flushed face with the colourful
cardboard
You looked up with the sweetest smile and asked, "What's funny?"
I replied with a gush in my voice saying "Nothing" as I reached out to gently
cup your face.

The meal was delicious, the atmosphere romantic and the music nostalgic
We left the place, walked hand in hand like we are in a slow dance
The street lamps in array as the moon displayed its magnificence
The stars flicked like chandeliers across the evening sky
You wrapped your arm around my waist and pulled me close to you as
passers-by looked in amazement.

Being held by you without a care in the world felt so enchanting
As I rest my head on your shoulders I whispered, "I'm yours and always."
You gently lifted my head with a loving stare piercing through my soul and
said, "And I am yours forever."
I looked back – my hand on your chest, I can hear our hearts' beautiful
rhythm
As the night bears witness to a one magical moment of a fairy-tale love to
remember.

Nov. 2014

Looking back

The year is ending – it has been a rollercoaster ride.
So much has happened – many have come and gone
I cannot fathom – some questions left unanswered and some has.

Remembering, some were filled with dismay – the fear of losing, the pain of
    loss and the feeling of surrender.
Days became weeks and then months, I came across the silver linings of
    life.

Down on my knees with only a prayer to hold on to – I let it lead me.
Reminiscing, I have found strength, but I have witnessed courage.
I have seen hope at each passing days and nights when life remained on
    a stand still.
I have felt faith through watching every pain and tear.

Looking back, I have learnt from someone's soul through their eyes.
I have been shown light and a glimpse of the rainbow.
I have sensed comfort through every fall and a hand through which I stand.

In my reflection, I have so much to thank for – I call my blessings.
I have a knit – may not be in the same place but tied tightly to reach
    another
I have angels – my special stars to shine brightly in the skies when I'm in the
    dark.

While contemplating, my heart is filled with thanksgiving.
I have my own compass to hold on to each step of every journey
I have a guide to get me through thick and thin . . . through joys and pain.

God is my North – the centre of my being
Family is my South -the love of my life and I turn to no matter what the odds
True friends – my West to which I hope I can lean on when I need to
Myself is the East – the balance to self, a walk to life and a gift of living.

Christmas, Dec 2014

So Many Things ...

There are so many things clouding over me
I want to tell you in different ways, to no avail
So many things I want to say for my head to open up
So many things, but then my heart could not utter
The many things I just want and need to.

There are things I keep on playing in my head
The words scrambled in different angles
I don't know which way to tell you
I can't find a chance, a space nor a time to say
Because my heart says another way.

So many things in my heart that feels pain
There's that emotion of turmoil and questions
I know in my heart you are real and pure
I know in your heart you are sincere and true
Yet there are things you do I don't understand.

There are many things you have said
Many things I consider and hold in my heart
Yet there are things you say so much but never do
The things you say differs from the things you do
Things you cannot see to change nor need to be.

Tonight laying down next to you, many things come to mind
Things I have asked my heart while my head thinks
I have asked my heart, "Are you feeling okay?"
My mind in a muddle, feeling lost in a battle
So many things I don't want to regret in the end
Tonight I want to ask, "Can you, out of many things I say make just one thing
    right?"

Jul 2015

Rainbows and Puddles

The clouds looking so sad as loneliness trace each line
The wind is gushing and every whisper shivers
I can feel its pain and the turmoil inside
The sky is like a blanket of grey with what's left of the light
It feels heavy as its tears are ready to let go.

Staring blankly from my window
The weather seems duplicating my emotions
I looked deeply into the darkness
Somehow, I want to find a glimpse of heaven
Somewhere I want to find a glimmer of a shadow.

I started reminiscing the moments of you and I
I recounted the times we had together – the good and the bad
When you were my company of pursuits and day dreaming
When you helped design my written ideas into pictures
When you swayed my goals and painted it into a reality.

I began to find myself smiling at the recollection of you
My tears flowing not because I am sad but because I feel blessed
I had you maybe for a short time but those were moments of true love
You've taught me how to dream and be inspired of simple things
You've showed me how to love patiently even if it takes time.

The rain has stopped and the sun's up to glitter and shine
I can see the rainbow as the white clouds covers the skies
I peeped through with a hope of seeing you once again – just this time
There I saw at the rainbow's edge – You staring back with that same look of
    love
There, I know that even up there you will still paint my dreams with me.

For my Shadow . . . .1 year on 10th Dec.
Always in my heart my fur baby

Dec 2015

When the snow fails to fall

When the snow fails to fall
The celebration seems like a fleeting glance
The festive season came to pass – glided and sailed away
It felt like a distant memory of a yesterday's dream.

When the snow fails to fall
The excitement of every game to play is hollow and distant
The anticipation of waiting is a lost battle and entangled in between
For that one special moment now becomes the same ordinary day.

When the snow fails to fall
Imagine the feeling of wintry mist as every laughter warms the air
Children playing snow angels as Mr Snowman smile in delight
With every grown-up join in the merriment as they clutch balls of snow to
    throw.

When the snow fails to fall
There is that little child's dream shifting to a mirage
Whispers of prayers heeding for a snowflake to drizzle
That tonight as they lay to sleep when they wake up a blanket of white
    covers every street.

When the snow fails to fall
There is that 'maybe' in every heart's wishes
As the sleigh in the corner waits for a joyride
A sigh is uttered, if not today 'maybe' then tomorrow I will dream again.

Christmas Vienna, Austria
Dec 2015

One Winter Holiday

A foggy morning enveloped the skies above me
Whilst walking along the streets of Christmas Market
The quiet and empty spaces seem so inviting as roasted chestnuts start to
　　fill the air
A few people coming and going, checking and nosing around
In every stand of little things and keepsakes up for last minute shopping.

The morning dew smells like fresh drops of winter
The chilly breeze bringing sweetness to each breath I take
Violins playing in every corner street as passers-by stop to listen
Holiday cheers unfolding as carols can be heard in every store and shop
That as the day breaks into noon, the once quiet place is filled with
　　harmonious titters.

The silence now broken with the festive sound of angels' choir
Strangers greeting one another as children smile from ear to ear
Traces of excitement in their eyes as they count the hours left to sleep
Lights surround from nook to nook as bells ringing to the wind's whispers
While Jolly Old St. Nick's rosy cheeks lifts the young and old into high spirits.

The winter tide radiate in every child and child at heart into dreaming
That every yearning is filled with the magic of love
There is that longing for beautiful surprises to look forward to
That as soon as Jack Frost bids farewell chances are, tomorrow hope
　　springs
For there's another winter break to await with pocketful of lists and a handful
　　of wishes to make.

Christmas Vienna, Austria
Dec 2015

A Shadow's Memory

One October day, someone gave me an old shoe box . . . something's
    moving
I wasn't sure what the occasion was but I was thankful for the gift . . . and
    curious
As I slowly opened the cover . . . there I saw a stare
Green eyes looking back . . . scared and questioning 'Who are you? Where
    am I?' At that moment, I knew you are mine.
You are one frightened creature . . . aloof and alone
You are one tiny living thing . . . who lived in fear and in so much pain
But from then, I promised you . . . you will be happy
From then, I told myself . . . you will be free
From then, until your last breath . . . you my little girl will be loved and always.
It took a lot of patience and time . . . for you to be near me
It took a lot of scratches and patches . . . for you to be held
It took a lot of courage and will . . . for you to come out from the dark
It took a lot of waiting and sneaking . . . for you to be seen out of your shell
When finally, the moment came, as I cuddled you close to my heart . . . you
    gave me your trust.
Two years on, I can tell you . . . I still cuddle you in my dreams
I still hear your purring as you nestle on my chest . . . I still hold you tight
I smile at every chance I think of you . . . that when I see other cats I know
    you're amongst them
I look at your pictures, I giggle at the memories of 14 years . . . of mischiefs
    and adventures
My Shadow, my little girl . . . no days are gone without you being missed
But knowing you're happy . . . that thought will keep the days going with you
    in my heart!

Remembering my muse, Shadow
Dec 2016

A Piece of Me

There is that moment in silence you want to seize time
There is that time in solitude you want to stop moving
There is that chaos in your head when chance becomes an experience
And that every chance it forms into a journey of life.
In my life's journey, I know I've made mistakes, but I learned to grow
In my daily living, I felt weak, yet I've found strength to stand up
In my everyday routine, I've struggled still I kept looking for challenges to test
  me
In my waking hours, I was about to quit but faith kept me going
And at each of these moments I have discovered how blessed I am and
  have always been.
At the start of each adventure I have found a life I belong
Together, we made promises and breathe that same oath
Together, we discovered our dreams and will thrive to build that drawn plan
Together, we unfolded the same hope and will hold on to fate
And together, we created a family – of friendship, love and a lifetime.
The pieces of recollections are values that bind my soul
The part of each travel are experiences that shaped me to who I am now
The steps I have taken are my chosen path no matter how hard or where it
  takes me
The decisions I have made are tests to my limits and boundaries
As each connection unfolds, another chapter of me opens to welcome the
  next story of myself and I.

Birthday
January 2017

Why, I Love You? (This is Us)

Why, I love you?
Because you annoy me and deliberately make it a point to annoy me any
    moment in time . . .
Because you make me smile at the way you do thoughtful gestures or even
    say stupid things . . .
Because you make me laugh every time you argue with the TV or the
    magazine you read just because . . .
Because you make me giggle whenever you talk to yourself of "how
    amazing I am" loudly making sure I hear it . . .
Because you just make me happy.

Why, I love you?
Whenever you say "You're safe" and wrap me so tight in your arms . . .
Whenever you tell me "You're a little trouble" and playfully pinch my cheeks . . .
Whenever you ask me "You need anything?" I know I'm going to be okay . . .
Whenever you feel I need some "me time" you still make sure I'm
    comfortable and warm . . .
Whenever you do, as long as you're there, I am happy.

Why, I love you?
With your strength and your sense of positivity, I find a rock and a shoulder to
    lean on . . .
With every hopes and dreams that we share means a journey of a lifetime . . .
With every blueprint of adventures drawn together means we will face it
    hand in hand . . .
With faith for whatever may be ahead of us means we work as a team – as
    one . . .
With you and I, we make it through – whenever or just because we are
    happy.
Simply, that way is why I love you!

For Ru
Valentine's Day February 2017

I am just different

In a box of skittles, you seem to find the colours of the rainbow
Amongst the colours each one has that special taste – acquired and not
Each piece has a sense of smell and aroma may it be sour or sweet
Each one of us will then pick first a favourite then the next best thing
Which one will you pick?
If blue can be a blueberry, a grape and a mix of a fig and a plum
Red a raspberry, a strawberry or could be a cherry in a bun
Green is either a honeydew, a kiwi and maybe as sour as a lime
Yellow as sweet as mangoes, a persimmon, a slice of lemon and
    pineapple pie
Orange will be just orange with some cape gooseberries and tray of
    apricots on the loose
Which one will you choose?
What I am saying is, whatever you pick – sweet, bitter or sour
Whichever you choose, will that change who you are?
Whenever you like a pickle or two and a sweet apple pie to chew
Is it about what you like to look amongst the cluster or a crate of its dew?
Or is it about how you feel and the mien of that moment in time?
In life we make our own choices – an extract of our sense and sensibilities
Every day when we make that choice would mean we take a chance of
    our eccentricities
In chances we find a moment to dare to plunge whatever the odds – we
    take the shot
In that moment when we dare, we feel different – we are curious and can
    be extinct
In being different we see a difference of who we are and what we can be –
    peculiar yet unique
And in a gallery of skittles there is a passionfruit flavoured from the horde of
    our rarity.

Jun 2017

2019

We start to ponder what is going to happen ... love, work, health ... all about life and living.

We relive our successes, our failures ... what we have lost, what we have achieved and what we have gained.

We make plans ... our so-called New Year's resolutions ... a drawn out plan of goals and objectives.

We think of adventures and a bucket list ... may be a travel to a different world ... learn a hobby or a language and a journey to the unknown to look forward to.

We begin to make dreams ... aspire for what we hope to have and to become a reality.

We start to reflect upon what was last year ... what it was, how it was supposed to be and where it ended.

Today, I have nothing but being thankful ... for having given another chance and another time ... to make precious moments and memories.

I have nothing but a silent prayer ... that whatever may come, I will have strength and a proven faith within ... to stand the test of time.

I have nothing but a clutch of hope, that life ... love ... and living will be way better than the last ... be the best I can be.

For whatever this year may bring ... I have nothing but a heart filled with so much love from a partner – an ally ... my rock and compass, a family ... my tower and my shield, and real true friends ... my guide and gentle conscience.

Hong Kong New Year
January 2019

Sometimes

Sometimes, I spend time looking for faults
At times, I look for failures along with a few disappointments
Many times, I look for something I did wrong – or some mistakes I have
    made
And most of the time I look for something I hopefully did just right.
Sometimes, I wonder and ask all the maybes I come upon
At times, I ask the should haves and should have beens I can recount
Many times, I ask myself the what ifs and what coulds I discover
And most of the time I ask the whys I can unravel and find the answer.
Sometimes, I imagine scenes that may happen or may not
At times, I imagine a role I could be playing – am I a hero or a villain?
Many times, I imagine I have written a play or a script of life
And most of the times I imagine it may become or may never come
Sometimes, I sit still just so I can keep my nagging thoughts linger
At times, I close my eyes so I can see a glimpse of a dream
Many times, I wish that at least a prayer will be answered
And most of the times I suppose my hopes may never be the same as
    yours
Sometimes, my ideas will not be your outlook
At times, my point of view to things will be your different perspective
Many times, my approach to life will not be your concept to living
And most of the times, my vision of an adventure will never be a facet of
    your quest.
Sometimes, along the way we will have that one moment
At some point in time, we find the same equation although have worked it
    out in a peculiar way
Many times, we compromise and concede to the reality of something
Yet, most of the times we will decide and draw a line of who we are and
    what makes us who we are and what we have become.

Hong Kong
January 2019

My Beautiful Remembrance

In the quietness of the evening, a memory of you filled me
I can see you looking at me, asking to whether I'm okay
I can see your stare, pushing me to just keep going
I can see in your eyes, telling me that I can do it
And I can see in your smile, promising me you will be there.
In the orange sunset, every story you used to tell us sent me shivers it makes
   me just smile
I can hear your voice filled with passion in every word
I can hear from your tone with courage yet there's that meekness
I can hear you speak with sincerity and wittiness even in sadness of your tale
And I can hear your whisper, with such comfort to keep me calm.
In the stillness of the dusk, I remember your songs that make my heart in
   joyous rhythm
I can hum the lullaby you used to sing us to fall asleep
I can chant the lyrics of the melody you sung when I was crying
I can whistle the hymns of your happy song to make me laugh
And I can still belt out our duet on my own knowing you're singing with me.
As the nightfall draws near, I pray you are watching over me
I close my eyes, that I can see you next to me
I close my eyes, that I can hear your voice say a little prayer for me
I close my eyes that I can listen to your lullaby and sing it with you
And that as morning comes, I wake up with warmth knowing in my heart
   you never have left.

For my Abuela
April 2019

Last Night's Rainfall

The rain didn't stop last night . . . just kept falling endlessly turning puddles into ponds

It seemed like the clouds had carried too much load . . . that it needed to cry

The louder the thunder . . . I could feel the pain of hearing it let go

The lightning struck to show its frustrations . . . the despair of being ignored

As the rain fell harder . . . the wind joined to chime its agony and misery.

I imagined myself standing outside . . . screaming along with the thunder

I am soaked . . . I am cold and shivering as the raindrops fall along with my tears

I want to talk . . . but I feel my significance is not relevant

My voice is beginning to croak . . . my shout is becoming a whimper

I want to keep crying . . . but inside of me is dry and empty.

I stared from my misty window looking for something . . . amid the darkness outside

I traced a shadow of maybes . . . that I will find answers to every doubt I have

My mind disputing with my heart . . . am I feeling regret or am I just confused?

My head throbbed from thinking too much . . . maybe from false aspirations

But my heart racing like lightning . . . maybe from a vow of passion

I sobbed harder and harder . . . that maybe there's an end to it

My hand on heart silently praying . . . that maybe when this is over, I will see a lamplight

My mind in surrender a whisper of faith . . . that maybe someone is hearing me

My breath of relief hides my resignation . . . that maybe somehow the storm will pass

As I closed my eyes my sleep will be a sign of clarity and calm from my entangled soul . . . my sodden spirit after a rainfall.

October 2019

Broken

It's past midnight . . . the dawn is awake and I'm here still up in bed thinking
I could hear my heart beating . . . my pulses throb like drums
My thoughts racing about anything . . . about something
My mind mapping out tomorrow . . . scribbles that I don't even know
There's a sense of dread and a handful of doubts . . . questions unanswered
Of what tomorrow brings . . . what I will be facing . . . will I make it through?
Tomorrow is another day . . . the day of a week of laughter
Yet there lies a torment of clouds and signs with tilted directions
The smile and the laughter . . . they're my mask to cover my vulnerabilities
    . . . my imperfections
As the silver lining clings and overwhelms my soul . . . my spirit hanging on
I want to shout but I can't as there are issues other than me . . . someone
    else is shouting
I want to say something, but my eyes see more pain than I have . . .
    somebody else is drowning
I guess I am lost . . . I am drowned . . . I am somewhere hidden in my own
    cocoon
I need to glue myself back as I am broken . . . shattered in fragments of
    myself.

*Dedicated to those suffering from mental health issues. I see you . . . I feel
you. Sending you love and hugs!*

Oct 2019

The call of Autumn

6:00 am I woke up to a soft chilly breeze . . . The sun is up but it's hiding from the array of dark clouds.

The warmth of my coffee cup and the aroma of the ground beans gave me a reason to fill my day.

Walking through the secret pathway, fallen leaves crushed at my every step as the squirrels are up to start their errands of collecting acorns and nuts

I could hear the birds chirp and singing to a melody of their own . . . a chant to say 'Hello' and 'How do you do?'

Looking up, the trees have begun to change its colour transforming into different shades and streaks

The yellow leaves flashing the golden rays of the sun while the orange cast like a tincture of the sunrise.

Leaves of brown are the hues of the forest . . . a painted copper and amber to welcome the equinox of autumn.

The season has changed, a refreshing sign of something . . . an existence and a reality of the present

Looking back . . . the perceived image appeared a distant view of yesterday

It felt like I have walked a thousand steps and ten thousand strides more to reach where I am.

From where I'm standing, I see a parallel space . . . a middle ground from what comes after today.

Turning around I headed to a reserved direction . . . an exclusive walkway of chosen identities

The road is restricting my movement and my options to access the trail . . . to a route of familiarity

I tried to cross and make my own track but somehow, I am entwined by the precept of tradition.

There is that notion that I am breaking custom . . . a ritual of old-fashioned habit

But the main aspiration is to balance the design . . . an exceptional drive to mend what is broken and revamp what is uplifting.

I pursued on my yearning . . . my passion to be distinctive from the rest whilst remaining grounded and unpretentious

Around me I see a small crowd who wears the same viewpoint . . . a vision
to create a better transformation

Within each character carries a striking component of mastery and
capabilities . . . an individuality of talents.

Contemplating upon my singularity, there is that glimpse of thought that
maybe things will be different . . . what if another can imagine the small
crowd's blueprint.

Examining . . . framing my own imagination, a script is written but for some
reason I cannot see the epilogue.

Then maybe, just maybe I may have to wait until the call of autumn has
ended for winter to arrive . . . a call of a new season to lead a new
direction.

Nov 2019

The whispers of a Christmas Wish

Christmas is drawing near . . . as midnight strikes the choir assemble to sing the joyous hymn of praise
The bells all set to vibrate the whole place with their ringing
Drummers in huddle to start the beat of our hearts with glee and cheers
Pipers piping as they march and dance along with every rhythm and melody
As children run outside to greet Santa on his sleigh with gifts he's bringing.
I smiled like a child while I sketch every scene and every move
There's that little kid at heart in me waiting for the snow to fall
There's that deeper prayer of white Christmas to wake up to
That the first snowfall of Christmas covers the world in white blanket
A cloak of hope and a quilt of love to comfort us all.
I play the picture in my head . . . a theatre of nothing but love and faith
The orchestra of angels serenading us . . . to hear the prayers in our trusting hearts
The stars glisten as Rudolf's red nose glimmers for us to believe . . . to see tomorrow
That somehow inside us we still wish for something . . . the gift we need
That somewhere we continue to dream . . . we pursue that dream we want.
Tonight, as we lay in bed in silence, we softly mumble our little wish
Tonight, as our eyes feel heavy, we count our every blessing with grateful hearts
Tonight, as we are deep in slumber . . . we see the facets of our desire
Tonight, as we dream . . . we reach a rainbow to whisper a prayer
That for tonight's stillness a wishing star will stop by to grant the innocent's sigh.

Merry Christmas to all little big kids!
Christmas 2019

Waiting for 2020 to unfold

The chill in the air beacons the sunlight to come out from hiding
The fog continues to sleep with unwillingness to rise up
The sky is grey as it shows little sign of light
The neighbourhood is quieter and subtle . . . a feel of laziness around
There are a few movements in the streets . . . as the day unfolds aside.
While this happens outside, inside is warm and cosy
The Christmas tree lights flicker like candlelit crystals
The smell of hot cocoa invites as the music soothes the tranquil soul
The clock ticks the minutes away with every second flying by
The year will soon end as the hour of every hour carries on.
Tracing my footsteps backwards . . . I looked at yesterday's episodes
I scanned through coincidences . . . peeped at my mistakes and missteps
I recalculated my decisions . . . if they were right or wrong
I glanced at my achievements . . . I did some impossibilities in my weakness
I peered at my gains . . . I have noticed old familiar faces, yet I have
     earned a lovely new crowd.
Recollecting my tales and stories, I learned resilience and patience
Reflecting on the challenges I had, I grew stronger and saw a different
     perspective
Reviewing my year, there were certainties, yet I stumbled on uncertainness
Remembering my false impressions of others, somehow made me
     reconsider my own judgement and not of others
Retrieving my individuality, I learned to share my talents and abilities openly.
At this moment, I am waiting for the year to end and the new to come
I am unsure of what is yet to come but I'm sure of what I have become
I take a step forward with a different vision . . . an unconventional insight
The remnants of bygone . . . I am taking pride as to how I made it here
I may not know what is coming in 2020 . . . but with unequivocal mind-set, I
     can only hope for better than the best!

New Year 2020

Withered

Woke up listening to the stillness of dawn . . . the silence feels deafening
Thoughts unfettered . . . turbulent emotions running through
Questions left unanswered searching for it to unravel in front of me
I am asking for a response maybe finding rebuttal of what tomorrow brings.

Tears started to trickle down unknowingly
A faint sob with forethought that someone from somewhere may hear
Clutched my chest while my other hand on my mouth to stifle the sound
But the heart heeds that no one will hear my cries.

Looking back I have made a momentum . . . achieved to keep going
The spirit is willing yet the body is un-obliging and resistant
The soul feels depleted . . . my heartbeat disconnected to the rhythm
Now all I see is darkness . . . an obscured facet.

Looking ahead I cannot see a light nor a glimmer
I was told it is just another chapter ready to be written
My heart is full of gratitude because somehow they see me in a different
    angle
But why am I feeling like a withered phantom and could no longer see what
    they see?

Why do I feel so desolated . . . unattached to what is now
Why do I feel blind . . . un-discerning to what is ahead
Why do I feel calloused . . . hardened from constant pain
Yet my spirit is yearning . . . to clamour a patch up of my withered heart in
    surrender.

August 2020

I am Silence

It's Saturday yet outside in quiet reverie – gentle and still
You hear nothing on each space for laughter to fill
The air is silent even the trees are unruffled
The birds are not singing – hushed and muffled
Squirrels are not coming out from their slumber
Have they enough acorn to last a yonder, I wondered

The silence is enchanting except it resembles to a magnetic mess
The stillness feels like the temper and sound of sullenness
Thoughts scatter solely while words bellow and scream
And the voices encased too shallow for an echo to gleam
The quiescent is suppressing yet it creates and contains serenity
The hush empties the mind to the depths of ones' soul – tranquil and
    sublime

As the eyes are becoming heavy – dazed like a trance
Listen to the heart's murmur and relish beat enhanced
Feel the sequence of a guitar's strand heightened inside you
Hear the hum of the wind as it coils and tints the morning dew
Slowly sway to the music as it weaves through in a steady glance
In your solace a heightened sensation calls – I am SILENCE!

December 2021

She may be "Boss" but she's simply Helen

Words can be uttered and hinged to describe you – of what you are
Others see you in a different way – on how you are
Some may outline you through their own lenses – just who you are
And a number can recount you in your meetings – from where you have
    been.
If you ask me on how I paint you – sketch you from the very start
Honestly, it has taken me awhile to find the exact words to draw you
Playing back memories through my mind is easy and uncomplicated –
    they're my stories to tell
And that summing-up those moments are the bond that shaped and
    made us.
The portrayal of you likens to a gemstone – precious and elegant
A diamond – solid and structured yet there's that transparency of your
    emotions, affections and spirit
Diamonds may have the highest hardness than any natural form – yet you
    cut and polish those you have met somehow made them whole
And in its rarest designs' diamonds are a paragon – like the essence of you.
There's no wonder why you glisten even in darkness and lightens the path
Your stability became our strength – a force that kept us steady and made
    us convalescent
Your compassion defines you – of what you stand for, of who you are and
    what you are
And in your fragility no matter what – you continue to glimmer for us to see
    a glint of light so we could shine.
Your sparkle is a pattern of hope and courage for us to aspire
Because of you the ideas became the blueprints of our vision and our
    archetype

You have created a foundation of true values, integrity and passion – an
  epitome of altruism
As we uproot and divide into different plains and places – you will find the
  testament of your design
The map of your legacy will continue to linger and ripple – it's your
  masterpiece, your gift and your pride.

*For Helen, my mentor, my special friend and my safe. Thank you for
making me who I am and who I can be. Happy Retirement*

Dec 2021

Twenty Twenty One

We leave 2021 behind some burden and save any lessons learnt

We've had our losses that we can't take back – painful and agonising to even think of

We've had gains to carry along – of finding ourselves with a realisation of what we have become

We have recognised our existence – of living not with tangibles but our true possessions.

The clock kept ticking – there's nothing we could do to turn back time – we've gathered regrets

Maybe I should have made more moments – memories to store and save

Memoirs of myself and of others – of those who we've met – kept along the way

Stories of our intimate warm times – the ones that we cherish and treasure.

Ten minutes to New Year we start to recollect – the good, the bad even the ugly

Through the mishaps – tears starts to trickle down while our hearts throbbing

Every beat we rethink – every rhythm we relive every minute to feel again

How it made us who we are today – on finding our strengths and discovering courage

Five more minutes we open and let the tears flow – became a cry of emotions

We weep for our sorrows and we scream for our failures – if only . . .

Yet through it all we find peace – we submit to it all with admission in surrender

Tomorrow we have gained more chances – possibilities to make choices and create changes

A minute becomes seconds – we reflect and close the chapter of yesterday

We realign the special moments – hold on to it even more – to the smallest detail

We raise our glasses- sing Auld Lang Sign as we hold on to hope with a smile

As the clock strikes to midnight a silent prayer is whispered – tomorrow is going to be a new day, it's a beginning.

Dec 2021

New pages – next chapter

Staring in front of a white sheet emotions disconnected – yet there is that sense of calm

The whiteness identical to a blanket of snow – untouched and unscathed

The serene piece felt placid – of empty thoughts

There's tranquillity of consciousness – a clarity of psyche.

It's the 1st day of the year – I have 365 days to find ways to produce a scheme

I have 8,760 hours to draft a plan – layout a storyboard of fate

Scanning through the pages it's clean and bare – my mind enticed to fill each sheet

The possibilities are endless but where to begin – how to launch an episode

It is easy to organise and plot a scene – for when tomorrow leads me to an unknown

What are the odds for a vision to unfold trapped to an unfinished business of yesterday?

All I see is a vacant landscape – a setting unfurnished with patches of surface

Underneath a part is yet to be created – a call for second chances, a sign of changes.

I have left behind the sadness – my melancholy of heartbreaks and despair

Looking up I'm taking with me blessings – tokens of strength to keep me balanced

Page by page – I started composing a capsule of hope with a leap of faith

That as the paragraph forms into another story my soul in surrender – my heart open.

The prelude: I wilfully overlooked the footnote – blinded with anger and distrust

Pushed away the very hands who purely believes in miracles – however big
  or small
That there are reasons I will never comprehend – though the answer may
  be as simple as ABC
But each time my heart throbs – I will take one step at a time – one beat of
  every moment I make
Another chapter may have ended – there will always be another book to
  begin.

New Year 2022